Dr. Stephen Covey's and Alan Mulally's Endorsements of *An Attitude of Excellence*

"Talk about a brilliant, inspiring, motivating book! Reading it—laced with powerful, practical examples—affirms and empowers you to *choose* success; to *choose* excellence; to see change and constant improvement as an ally instead of a fearsome enemy; [and] to choose a complementary team style where strengths are made productive and weakness made irrelevant because of the strengths of other team members. Intertwining personal and organizational/cultural development is so vital and beautifully illustrated throughout. What an illuminating, uplifting read! I can 'hear' and 'feel' Dr. Willie entertaining as well as educating."

—Dr. Stephen R. Covey, author of *The 7 Habits of Highly Effective People* and *The 8th Habit: From Effectiveness to Greatness*

"Dr. Willie Jolley has written a powerful new book that speaks to the impact of an attitude of excellence by every member of our teams. Our attitude of excellence creates a high-performance smart and healthy 'working together' culture that pulls everyone together around a compelling vision, comprehensive strategy, and relentless positive implementation for the benefit of all the organization's stakeholders. Share this with every member of your team!"

—Alan Mulally, former CEO of Ford Motor Company and Boeing Commercial Airplanes

More Praise for *An Attitude of Excellence*

"Willie Jolley is a master at guiding and motivating people to achieve success at home and in the workplace. This book shares the principles and tenets that he has put to good use during his career. Study them and apply them in your life."

—Dr. Nido Qubein, president of High Point University and chairman of Great Harvest Bread Company

"My friend Willie Jolley is one of the most positive, buoyant, and talented people I know. He understands the power of attitude and how to use it for personal and professional success. Listen to Willie and read his book if you want to soar higher on the wings of an excellent attitude."

—Mark Sanborn, award-winning speaker and author of
The Fred Factor, *You Don't Need a Title to Be
a Leader*, and *The Encore Effect*

"*An Attitude of Excellence* is a book that I believe will become a classic self-help book because attitude affects everything in our lives! Positive or negative attitudes become self-fulfilling prophecies. A must-read book for anyone committed to a quest for excellence in their personal and professional lives!"

—Dr. Tony Alessandra, NSA Speakers Hall of Fame motivational speaker and coauthor of *The Platinum Rule*

"*An Attitude of Excellence* is a dead-on reflection of Willie Jolley, a friend who is smart, positive, and caring . . . You buy the book, and you end up taking Willie Jolley home. What a deal!"

—T. Scott Gross, author of *Positively Outrageous Service*

"This book is powerful! In this book, Willie Jolley focuses on core organizational development issues—in an outstanding way! I know firsthand that this message can create a 'WOW' impact on your team!"

—Carlos J. Saldana, director of MCCS-US Marines in Okinawa, Japan

"When I thought about a way to inspire my organization, I looked at a number of business books and a number of personal development books . . . but then I got hold of *An Attitude of Excellence*, which was both in one book! And the response by my team has been incredible!"

—Eric Cevis, senior vice president and group president of Verizon Partner Solutions

"If you are in the hospitality industry, or any industry where you serve customers, this should be required reading for people at all levels of your organization. Dr. Willie Jolley is a master storyteller who is able to use words to captivate readers and motivate them to improve their performance and productivity. The anecdotes and ideas found in *An Attitude* of Excellence will inspire your team to wow and serve your customers with a positive attitude and commitment to excellence each and every day!"

—Doug Ridge, area general manager at the Gaylord National Resort and Convention Center

"The concept of an attitude of excellence is essential to ensure positive forward movement in business and life. I have bought boxes of the book and I have given this book to team members, new hires, and also to my son along with his high school friends! This book works!"

—Gail Smith-Howard, general manager at Hyatt Regency Washington

"What an incredible book! I have used *An Attitude of Excellence* with three different organizations that I have led. One had an existing culture of excellence, one was creating a new culture of excellence, and the last was blending 2 cultures that were radically different. An attitude of excellence challenges every reader to show up and expect to win. We were able to create cultures where winning was not just enough, it was the margin of victory that mattered . . . a 2–1 victory was not as fun as 15–1! The principles of this uplifting, inspiring, and entertaining book led to the most effective motivational tool that I have witnessed in my career. This book inspires the reader to hold themselves accountable at work, at home, and in the silence of their thoughts. We could see responses from team members when asked 'How are you doing?' go from 'I am good' to 'I am excellent!' The team members held each other accountable and no one wanted to be the weak link and disappoint other department heads. The ability of the organization to generate significant amounts of discretionary effort, it is that incremental effort that is made by each individual in the organization when no one is watching! Swing for the fences, expect to win, fail fast, and believe that you can win by a wide margin. The oxygen is very thin at this level of success but Willie Jolley's principles will help you enjoy the sweetness at the top of the mountain. Enjoy and get ready to shake and bake!"

—Tom Raponi, former vice president of GM
Cox Media, KTVU/KICU/WFXT

"Our sales team really enjoys the extra inspiration Willie Jolley's book provides in helping us to stay focused and never lose sight of our goals and mission. This book has impact! It helps us to remember the basics and run the play, and play to win!"

—Nancy Terry, senior vice president of US Fitness

"I read *An Attitude of Excellence* and it was so impactful that I have been sharing with my team members in both our locations in Maryland and

Georgia. This is the book that I have been praying for to help us grow our church. It inspires, informs, and motivates our people to excellence! I was so filled up by the wisdom in the book that I shared it with the people in my church. The result was that we saw an immediate positive response after people read the book! I highly recommend this book! It will change you, your people, and your organization!"

—Deron Cloud, lead pastor at the Soul Factory Church

"We had Dr. Willie Jolley to speak for our team and he was terrific. Then we decided to get copies of *An Attitude of Excellence* to reinforce the learning . . . and our team has been truly inspired by the book! We have seen tremendous growth in our people and their productivity! I highly recommend this book!"

—Tony Taylor, president of US Property Solutions Group

"Dr. Willie Jolley has written an incredible book that has helped our people to grow exponentially. He gives practical tips to grow our customer-centric service culture, as well as to grow our people individually. We love his concept that great people give great service, good people give good service, mediocre people give mediocre service, and negative people will kill your organization! We want great service, so we are using this book to grow the greatness in our people! Thank you Dr. Jolley!"

—Bishop Rivers S. Taylor, Jr., pastor of Bethlehem Judah Ministries in Newport News, VA

"My friend Dr. Willie Jolley has written a book that is going to blow your socks off! He is not only one of the most positive people on the planet but helps you and your team to grow your positive thinking and positive attitude! Read this book, then re-read it, then share it with everyone you know . . . because everyone needs an attitude of excellence!"

—Wally Amos, founder of Famous Amos

An Attitude of Excellence

Other books by Dr. Willie Jolley

A Setback Is a Setup for a Comeback

Turn Setbacks into Greenbacks

It Only Takes a Minute to Change Your Life!

Make Love, Make Money, Make It Last!
(co-authored with Dee Taylor-Jolley)

The ABC's of Achievement (digital)

An Attitude of Excellence

Get the Best from Yourself,
Your Team, and Your Organization

DR. WILLIE JOLLEY

BenBella Books, Inc.
Dallas, TX

Excerpt on pages 74 reprinted from *Get More Referrals Now* by Bill Cates, author of *Beyond Referrals* and *Radical Relevance*, published by McGraw-Hill Professional, 2004. Used by permission. All rights reserved.

Unless otherwise stated, scripture quotations are from the ESV Bible (The Holy Bible, English Standard Version), copyright © 2001 by Crossway, a publishing ministry of Good News Publishers. Used by permission. All rights reserved.

Unless otherwise stated, all photos are courtesy of Dr. Willie Jolley's personal collection.

BenBella Books, Inc.
10440 N. Central Expressway, Suite 800
Dallas, TX 75231
www.benbellabooks.com
Send feedback to feedback@benbellabooks.com

Printed in the United States of America
10 9 8 7 6 5 4 3 2 1

Library of Congress Cataloging-in-Publication Control Number: 2018018001
9781946885401 (trade cloth)
9781946885593 (electronic)

Copyediting by J. P. Connolly
Proofreading by Chris Gage and
    Cape Cod Compositors, Inc.
Text design by Publishers' Design
    and Production Services, Inc.

Text composition by PerfecType, Nashville, TN
Cover design by Bradford Foltz
Jacket design by Sarah Avinger
Printed by Lake Book Manufacturing

Distributed to the trade by Two Rivers Distribution, an Ingram brand
www.tworiversdistribution.com

Special discounts for bulk sales (minimum of 25 copies) are available. Please contact Aida Herrera at aida@benbellabooks.com.

*This book is dedicated to my wife and life partner,
Dee Taylor-Jolley, who continues to inspire
and encourage me to live my dreams and to help
others around the globe to live their dreams!*

CONTENTS

PREFACE

Attitude is just an eight-letter word, yet it has such a big impact on your life and your success. And excellence is a ten-letter word that can multiply your reputation tenfold in the marketplace.

These two main words make up this book's title—*attitude* and *excellence*. They are wonderful words in themselves, but together they can describe something exceptional. From the first time I thought of the words together—"attitude of excellence"—I was intrigued. This concept completely captivated me, and from the very first moment I wrote it on my idea notepad, I was inspired. The more I looked at this simple combination of words, the more I was struck by the concept. I was particularly struck by the fact that this concept combines two words that are widely used to express concepts that many of us say we want to pursue but that we often do not pursue with vigor! We talk about "the power of positive thinking" and how "attitude determines altitude," yet most of us do very little to actually grow our "attitude muscle." Attitude is a mindset and it is *why* we do what we do.

Likewise, we hear people talk about "excellence," but again, we do not always run after it with passion. Excellence is the quality or state of being outstanding and superior and it is *how* we do what we do.

After reflecting on the phrase "attitude of excellence," I realized that something was still missing in this title. I wondered, why would it be worth the extra effort to pursue excellence? What would be the payoff for pursuing an attitude of excellence? What would be the result of this work? The answer was that the payoff is when you achieve a level where you are considered to be one of the best, where you have been able to achieve a level of greatness! That goal would make the demanding pursuit of excellence worth it. That is why I start this book with several pages about the will to win and achieving greatness.

An Attitude of Excellence gives people within organizations a new perspective on the impact each individual can have on the long-term success of an organization. It will help today's workforce position itself for long-term employment, even in these changing and challenging times. And it will help organizations to not just survive, but also thrive through tough times.

This book is the culmination of many years of study, research, and personal experience that I learned from working with, and interviewing, some of the leading business leaders, personal development experts, and thought leaders across the globe. This book has been an ongoing, multiyear work in progress, which has expanded and grown as my thinking and learning has expanded and grown. Somewhat like a cathedral, where many of the great cathedrals take decades to complete, this book has been a part of my life for many years, taking a long time to complete, yet I am extremely excited about the result!

The original version of this book was written as a gift for my clients. I had been traveling around the country speaking to organizations about attitude and excellence, and lessons I had learned while working with outstanding companies like Ford Motor Company (during its amazing comeback from the brink of bankruptcy to being able to reject a government bailout during a major recession). The original version of *An Attitude of Excellence* elaborated on what I was saying to these organizations specifically about the importance of attitude and excellence for success. And the more I shared the lessons, the more clients asked about putting them into a book. So I listened and moved forward on giving them the lessons in book form.

In fact, it was one of my earlier books that led me to the connection at Ford in the first place. A Ford executive had heard me speak and bought my book *A Setback Is a Setup for a Comeback*.

Dr. Willie Jolley visits with Ford Motors' CEO at the time, Alan Mulally.

He then recommended me to work with Ford in its comeback. From that book reaching the right person at the right time, I was able to be a part of a historic experience that helped an American icon to survive and thrive and helped me to grow as a person and as a thinker. Plus, I learned some incredible secrets about the power of excellence!

I worked with Ford for three years and witnessed an amazing example of excellence in action. I watched how Ford's then-CEO, Alan Mulally, transformed Ford from a company that some were predicting would go out of business to a financially thriving company that went on to be named "America's most inspirational brand"!

From this Ford experience, I learned a number of lessons in how to navigate an organization, especially through some really tough times. First, from Mulally I learned the necessity of having a big, bold vision. Mulally's vision was to not only save Ford, but also to see it prosper. He focused daily on his dynamic plan to turn Ford around. When I visited him in his office in the Ford headquarters building in Dearborn, Michigan, he showed me a poster that was an advertisement originally printed in 1925 in the *Saturday Evening Post*. The painting in the ad was called *Visions of Tomorrow*, and the headline underneath was "Opening the Highways to All Mankind." The printed message of the poster stated that Ford Motor Company wanted to focus on serving people, and in doing so, the company must be large in scope (and thinking) and have a great, committed purpose. Mulally shared with me that Henry Ford used that concept to build Ford initially, and how Mulally was inspired by the advertisement to rebuild the new Ford. The advertisement truly gave an upbeat feeling of positivity and hope!

This also related to the second thing I learned from Mulally: the power of staying hopeful and positive, in life and in an organizational environment. Mulally remained upbeat throughout the turnaround, even in the toughest moments. He said we must think positive thoughts, speak positive words, and take positive action toward our goals, and do so each and every day. Both at Ford and elsewhere, I have seen that excellence is typically the result of forethought and planning, and that it is critical to have positive thinking and positive expectations. Then you must work hard to maintain that positive attitude, especially in the midst of challenges and adversity!

Third, from Mulally I learned the impact of being relentless in the pursuit of excellence. There were numerous accounts of people who told him that his plan was not going to work and that he should scale down his ambitions. Yet, he believed Ford could come out of this challenge better than it had been before the challenge began. He also empowered the Ford team to be relentless in the execution of the daily details. He pushed the team members to be honest in their evaluations and in their progress or in the problems they were having in reaching the goals. He taught them to rely on the data and to be honest in interpreting the numbers—no hiding the truth and no heads in the sand. He instructed them to face the problems and then work together to fix them. In the past, many people at Ford had not been forthright when they had problems, feeling that this was the only way to protect their positions. Mulally got them to understand that when excellence becomes the norm, then everyone can be honest, and therefore everyone will benefit.

Lastly, I learned from Mulally about the importance of working as a team. He knew how to pull people together to work as a unit. Ford had been known as a place where everyone was concerned about their own survival, not realizing that their own survival was connected to the success and survival of the company. Ford was also known as a place that was ruthlessly competitive; everyone was out for themselves. A written account of a McKinsey interview described it like this: "Ford was a crawl over each other, dog eat dog culture, and Mulally inspired them to work together, and to go from dog eat dog to a dog sled team that pulled together!"

Even though I played a small part in Ford's amazing comeback, the impact it had on my life and business was huge. I learned lessons about excellence in real time that empowered my thinking. After Ford's comeback I was mentioned in an article about how I helped Ford, and the same day the article was published I got a call from General Motors. The gentleman who called said, "If you can help Ford, you can help us!" I went on to work with GM, then many other companies called. I went on to work with many Fortune 100 companies like Walmart, Verizon, Prudential, Marriott, Johnson & Johnson, Procter & Gamble, Dell Computers, Hyatt, Coca-Cola, Comcast, Cox, McDonald's, Fannie Mae, Raytheon, Xerox, Nordstrom, Enterprise, and the list continued to grow. As I visited these different companies I continued to observe and learn, and continued to grow my thinking about excellence so I could help others to create their own amazing stories of excellence.

After a couple years of visiting and learning from all these super-successful companies I got a call from one of my clients who asked me to prepare a speech on what I had learned about leadership and excellence from all these Fortune 100 companies. I developed a speech on attitude and excellence, and the speech was so well received that my client asked me to come back and do more programs on the topics of attitude and excellence for more of his people. Then he shared the concept with his peers and the response was the same: Could I come and share it with their people? And there was one more interesting observation. As mentioned earlier, each time I shared the speech, my clients would ask for my notes. I decided to share the notes in book form and offer it as a thank-you gift to my clients for inviting me to speak to their teams. This is how the idea of this book as a gift book evolved.

As I was finalizing the notes into the finished book for my clients, however, I was faced with a challenge. How could I pack everything into one book when there are both professional growth and personal growth components to what I wanted to share?

I knew that the best way to grow an organization is to grow the people who make up the organization, and I knew that the greater the people in the organization, the greater the products and services that the organization brings to the marketplace. I knew that great organizations rely on having great people throughout their organizations. Finally, I knew that great organizations always focus on getting great people and that it is imperative to have great people at every level of the organization, because a holistic experience of greatness was essential from top to bottom and from bottom to top. It is imperative to have great people throughout the organization. Why? Well, I have said for years that "great people tend to give great service, good people tend to give good service, and mediocre people tend to give mediocre service—and negative people will kill your organization!" Also I share that "the more excited and focused on excellence that the people in an organization are, the harder they work to continue the success of the organization."

So, as I considered a book for professional organizational development in creating a culture of greatness, I knew I also needed to help the individual people in the organization grow their personal success. I finally decided to write two books, one for the professional development of the people involved and the other for their personal development. Then I wondered what it would be like if I combined the two books into one exciting book.

Once I finished a draft of the combined book, I started sending galley copies to my clients and asking for their thoughts. Each client did the exact same thing: They called and said they had read it and loved it, and then they immediately ordered copies for all their employees. Before long they were sharing the book with their friends and I was getting more and more orders for books. And this was a book that was not "officially" out. It was not in bookstores nor available in the normal book channels. It was only a book for my clients. I knew one day it would need to come out "officially." So after multiple print runs and thousands and thousands of copies of the "unofficial" version, I am happy to announce that you hold in your hands the official version of *An Attitude of Excellence: Get the Best from Yourself, Your Team, and Your Organization*! Plus, this new version has lots of great new information that I have learned since I wrote the original version years ago. And we also now have an online portal where I continue to share new information that you can access at your convenience. You can access the latest and greatest information at www.attitudeofexcellence.com.

Incidentally, the endorsement gracing this book's cover, written by the late author Stephen R. Covey, is one I received

Dr. Willie Jolley and Dr. Stephen Covey in Sydney, Australia, where they were the featured speakers for one of the largest real estate sales conferences in the world.

years ago for the "unofficial" book. There's an interesting story about how I got his endorsement.

Some years ago, I was speaking at an event in Australia, where the other featured speaker was Dr. Stephen R. Covey, author of the bestselling *The 7 Habits of Highly Effective People*. I told his assistant that I had a manuscript I was working on that I thought he would like and that I wanted to get an endorsement quote if he liked it. She replied, "Sorry, but no! He doesn't do quotes any longer." I tried a few more times with her, but each time it was "Sorry . . . no!"

Then, that night in the hotel fitness center, I was finishing my workout when who came in but Dr. Covey! He sat on the stationary bike next to me. So instead of calling it a day, I made myself ride another hour on the bike so I could talk to him! During that hour, we talked about life and family and how we both loved music and people who we both knew. He told me he was friends with my friend Gladys Knight, whom I had toured with on the Music and Motivation Dream Team Tour, and we both talked about her kindness. We talked about our marriages and how we both were in the "over-married club" because we married women who were smarter than us. After an hour of talking and developing a friendship I told him about my book, and he said, "Send it to me!" He gave me his personal email, and I sent it. True to his word, he emailed me an endorsement for the book. This story shows how having faith, staying positive, and not giving up can lead to great results!

INTRODUCTION:
THE WILL TO WIN

How the Best Rise Above the Rest

Finally, beloved, whatever is true, whatever is honorable, whatever is just, whatever is pure, whatever is lovely, whatever is commendable, if there is any *excellence* and if there is anything worthy of praise, think about these things.

—PHILIPPIANS 4:8, EMPHASIS ADDED

Excellence is making a commitment to do the right thing, at the right time, in the right way; to do some things better than they were ever done before; to be courteous; to be an example; to work for the love of work; to anticipate requirements; to develop resources; to recognize no impediments; to master circumstances; to act from reason rather than rule; to be satisfied with nothing short of our very best!

—THE MARSHALL FIELD COMPANY

As we begin this journey I want to ask you some preliminary questions: "Do you want to win—*really* win—both professionally and personally? Do you want greater success? Do you want more in the future than you have had in the past? Would you like to make more money in the future than you have made in the past?"

I believe most people actually do want to win, but often they are not adequately positioned to win. When I ask these questions at the beginning of my speeches, I always get the same response: "Yes, I really want to win!" That is good. But there is a critical follow-up question, which is, "How *badly* do you want to win?" In other words, are you willing to do what is uncomfortable? Are you willing to stretch? Are you willing to do some things differently, and to do some different things? Are you *willing to change* in order to win?

If you answered "Yes" to any of these questions, then continue to read on. If you answered "No," then continue to read on anyway! I am sure you will gain a new perspective in this book that will positively impact your thinking, possibly for a lifetime! (I also encourage you to take the Attitude of Excellence Test. Go to www.attitudeofexcellence/test and rate yourself on a 1 to 5 scale to see how you rate!)

• • •

This book has two major objectives: to grow mindset and skillset. Mindset is attitude (why you do what you do) and skillset is excellence (how you do what you do). It is organized into two parts. The first part of the book is about how to create an organizational culture of excellence. I look at what the best organizations do and the five secrets that guide their success. Think of this first part as an organizational development and professional development guide that focuses on the five key components necessary to create a culture of excellence. In these chapters I concentrate on ideas that can help an organization excel and improve performance, productivity, and profits. Throughout this part, I share secrets I have learned while working with leading-edge organizations around the world. The secrets provide insights for you to use to expand your thinking. They are things the best companies know and do, and they are things you can do too, even if you are an organization with only a few people or even a single person growing a business. I suggest ways you can quickly implement these secrets to personally improve your business today.

The second part of the book is about how to grow yourself personally along with your future. I look at five simple steps that you can take to develop a life of excellence at work, at home, and in your community activities. Think of this second part as a personal development guide. It focuses on the necessary building blocks for personal development so that an individual, whether in a company or working alongside other companies, can make a greater impact as part of a winning team. If the people who work in the organization can become better individually, and can express that improvement in their day-to-day activities, then that organization can start to see rapid improvement because of the power of synergy and momentum. But what's good for the company is also good for the individual. I have found that people who are happier at home tend to be happier at work, and people who have drama at home tend to have drama at work. So this book is designed to help you have more success, less drama, and a whole lot more fun both at work and at home!

So, if you are really serious about achieving that type of success, then this book is for you! Are you somebody who wants to win? Are you someone who wants to be the best and rise above the rest? If so, keep reading, because that's what this book is all about—having the right attitude, striving for excellence, and achieving a level of greatness so you're on par with the best of the best and thereby enabled to get the benefits that come with being the best.

The commonality of both parts is the quest for five-star success, whether personally or professionally. Have you ever thought about why it is that some organizations consistently stand head and shoulders above their competition? Or how it is that some organizations reach world-class or five-star status, while others are never able to grasp the golden ring? The second-tier organizations often work very hard, but five-star success eludes them. I was intrigued by that dilemma, so I set out to find the answer.

The Secret Sauce

I sought out organizations with five-star ratings, interviewed their top people, and found that all of these companies had very similar environments. Plus, as a speaker, I receive invitations to speak at top organizations around the world, and as a result I have been able to observe, investigate, and collect information about the principles that separate the outstanding companies from their competitors. I learned that the top-tier people and organizations had developed a culture, an environment that inspired and embraced an attitude of excellence.

I noticed two key things. First, the pursuit of excellence was a consistent guiding principle in the personal and professional lives of the people at successful organizations—they were always striving to be better, to be more excellent. I call this the will to win. Once an organization knows what it is aiming for, it must focus on the *how* part—how to achieve that culture of excellence—and that's what part one of the book is all about.

Second, I discovered that there were five things these great organizations all did. I call these things the five secrets to organizational success. The following are the five things the best of the best do:

1. They recognize the power of dynamic leadership development and they develop leaders *at every level* of the organization.
2. They are proactive about change, passionately embracing it so the organization can *grow* through the changes, not just *go* through them.
3. They promote a "teamwork makes the dream work" mindset where everyone is an MVP.
4. They don't stop at great customer service. They know it's essential to absolutely "WOW!" their customers.
5. They nurture a world-class, winning attitude among all employees, where *everyone expects to win* every single day.

These secrets work for our personal lives too. We'll look more at our personal lives in part two of the book, where I give you five steps you can take for personal transformation. As an individual, if you want five-star success, you, too, need the will to win.

Are You Known for Excellence or Mediocrity?

Many people speak of the importance of branding, which is a popular concept used to discuss how people should position themselves in the minds of others, and it is essential to create a personal brand of excellence. In regard to personal services, it is more commonly thought to build a reputation. So, to increase our income, it is important to focus on the power of creating a reputation for excellence. The brand, or reputation, for excellence is one of the hallmarks of those who succeed in life and business. Developing a reputation for excellence is a way to build our personal brand and increase our personal wealth!

History offers us many examples of people and organizations that had quick success and made money in the short term but could not sustain that success. The reason they could not sustain their success is that they did not make a commitment to excellence. They were willing to take shortcuts, and some of those shortcuts proved to be their undoing! Developing a brand, or reputation, for excellence is the best insurance for long-term wealth and success.

Steve Jobs, the cofounder of Apple Computer and Pixar, and the creator of iTunes, the iPod, the iPad, and the iPhone, changed the world by refusing to settle for mediocrity. Steve Jobs is considered to be one of the greatest innovators ever. He expected excellence in everything he worked on and pushed everyone, including himself, to be excellent and to create excellent products. He created products that people didn't even know they needed, but once they had them they could not live without them. He created revolutionary products that began as an idea and he stayed focused on them until they came to realization, and he always pursued every project with an attitude of excellence.

Jobs created products that were not only excellent in terms of their functionality, but also excellent in terms of their appearance. In a December 2003 interview with *Rolling Stone* magazine, he said, "When you're a carpenter making a beautiful chest of drawers, you're not going to use a piece of plywood on the back, even though it faces the wall and nobody will see it. You'll know it's there, so you're going to use a beautiful piece of wood on the back. For you to sleep well at night, the aesthetic, the quality, has to be carried all the way through."

Steve Jobs said something that continues to inspire me and push me to keep raising up my pursuit of excellence. He said: "Make the commitment to be a yardstick of quality! Some people are not used to an environment where excellence is expected! You be that example!"

Steve Jobs did not settle for mediocrity in his work, and neither can you. In a time of endless competition, nanosecond change, and economic uncertainty, it is critical to look to the long term and recognize that excellence is essential to greater personal and professional success. Being excellent in our jobs is essential for continued employment in the workforce, and for job promotion, and it's how you become known as someone who sets the bar—someone who's the yardstick of quality—in an industry. Excellence not only matters, but it makes the biggest difference in your long-term success.

No More Job Security

Today's workplace is no longer the work environment of our parents' generation. The workplace that your parents experienced has dramatically changed. There was a time when a person could get a job out of high school and stay in that job until they retired. Those days are long gone. The concept of lifetime job security is a thing of the past. Many of us were encouraged by our parents to go to school, get a good education, get a good job, and stay there until retirement. Today, however, we routinely hear about people who went to school, received a good education, and found a good job, only to lose it for reasons that they could not control.

Over the last few years we have heard story after story of layoffs, downsizing, and reorganizations that disrupt lives and shake people to their core. There are people close to retirement after years of dedicated service to a company, who due to circumstances beyond their control have lost their jobs. There are workers who, through no fault of their own, have lost their jobs because of changing economic conditions. They got caught in a numbers game. Companies that once were the market leaders, like Woolworth Department Stores, Circuit City, Sears, or Lehman Brothers, lost market share and trimmed their workforce or decided to close up shop for good.

In today's rapidly changing marketplace, there is no such thing as job security! No one can guarantee you will stay employed or stay in good standing in your present position. There could be a change in the direction of the company, or the direction of the industry, or the economy. Numerous scenarios beyond your control could impact your present employment.

But I have some good news! You will always greatly enhance your job security by developing a reputation for excellence, and even if you're let go amid the downsizings, rightsizings, and restructurings, if you've developed a reputation for excellence, like cream rising to the top, so will you in regards to getting another job. Workers who have developed a reputation for excellence are always the first to get hired by other companies. Why? Employers are always looking for talented individuals with a desire for excellence and a great attitude. They are always looking and waiting for excellent people to become available. The key, though, is to develop a reputation for excellence *before* you need it. As the old saying goes, "It is always best to dig your well before you are thirsty!"

So while there is no such thing as job security, excellence is the best remedy for staying employed in a changing and challenging marketplace.

Even Your Competitors Take Notice

I didn't really grasp the full significance of this phenomenon of excellent workers rising to the top until I was older and saw examples of people who always seemed to be in demand, even when others were losing their jobs. One example is the situation a friend went through when the owner of the company she worked for decided to retire and close the company. My friend was concerned because she was not sure how she would fare after being at the same company for a number of years. She thought she would have a difficult time finding another job since she was older and most of the workforce in her industry was so much younger. Yet, as soon as the word got out that her company was closing, she was bombarded with offers—including offers from competitors who knew of her reputation for excellence and wanted to have her on their team!

Another example is my childhood friend Biddy. She and I grew up in the same neighborhood and even went to the same college, the American University, in Washington, DC. During her sophomore year, Biddy fell in love, got married, left school because she needed the money for an apartment, and started working in the federal government as an entry-level employee. Her job was to answer phones and make photocopies of policy manuals. Yet she did it with such zeal that she quickly became a hit in the office. She would answer the phones and say, "It's a great day! How can I serve you?" She would do that from 9 o'clock in the morning until 5 o'clock in the evening. She would even answer the phone with the same enthusiasm after hours while she waited for her husband, Dexter, to pick her up after work. She often worked an extra hour every day, never looking at the clock, and always focusing on what needed to be done!

When she was asked to make photocopies, she would make them with such precision that many people in the office thought they had been sent out to a printer. When she made copies of the training manuals, she made an extra one that she could read at night so she could create a list of ideas to share with her supervisor. She would always say, "If these make sense to you, please feel free to use them. If not, just throw them in the trash." Even though she enjoyed her job, she often talked about going back to college and finishing her degree as soon as she and her husband could get their finances straightened out.

Biddy quickly moved from an entry-level position (GS-2) to that of an administrator (GS-7) before she became pregnant with her first child. When she returned from maternity leave, she showed the same spirit of excellence. She would answer the phones with enthusiasm, even after hours. She would still make photocopies with a precision that astounded the staff, continuing to make one for herself and jotting down ideas that she thought might be helpful for the team. She moved from a GS-7 up to a GS-10, and then she became pregnant again.

This time, childcare costs for two children were very expensive, so Dexter and Biddy decided it would be more cost effective if she stayed home. She stayed at home for a few years, but once the kids were of school age she started the process of going back to work. A federal government job freeze proved a challenge for Biddy this time; and the only job available was at entry level (GS-2), answering phones and making photocopies of the policy manuals, where she had began years earlier! Needless to say, Biddy took the job and went back to work with the same enthusiasm and same work ethic as before.

One day when she answered the phone, the person on the other end was a voice she had not heard in many years. It was her very first supervisor when she was just entering the workforce after her first year in college. He was shocked to hear her voice on the other end of the phone line. He told her that he had been trying to find her. He spoke of how he had never forgotten her diligence and her positive attitude. He had raved to others over the years about her attitude of excellence, and that her positive attitude had become a model he shared with new employees. He explained that he was now the director of a new agency and he was looking for a special assistant. He wondered if she would be willing to leave her present job to come work with him. Of course, that would entail a raise that was outside the dimensions of the freeze. Plus, she would have a staff of people to supervise! She giggled and said, "Excuse me, sir . . . when do I start?" She took the job and was again excellent in the position, and again she still went the extra mile. She had a staff of people to support her, but when others didn't quickly answer the phone, she would pick it up herself and say, "It's a great day! How can I serve you?"

Biddy continued to show that excellence truly is the best job security and job advancement strategy. She became the

Director of Policy and Programs for the Department of Energy and continued to pursue excellence, even after she retired. She would get assignments to share her mindset of excellence with new employees and literally would get job offers every week. Recently, I spoke at a government agency where she used to work. When I mentioned I knew her, the staff raved about how she had been such a bright light and how her enthusiasm for excellence had been contagious throughout their organization. They all talked about her attitude of excellence!

And by the way, when her first child graduated from college, so did Biddy! She graduated the same day. Biddy had found a way to go back to college while working and raising her children. When I asked Biddy the secret to her success, she told me, "I learned that excellence offers no excuses but rather focuses on getting the job done, even in the midst of challenging situations." She said, "There is no substitute for excellence. It is always the best job security!"

Dream Team Players

This taking notice of excellent workers can be seen in other areas, too, such as the sports industry. Imagine that after winning a world championship in basketball, a new ownership group bought the latest winning championship basketball team. (Get a picture in your mind of the most recent NBA championship team.) Next, get a picture in your mind of the star player on that team. Then imagine that a crazy billionaire offered the current owner twice the value of the team and the current owner decided to take the money. Now imagine that the new crazy owner decided that he wanted to start over with his own group of players and coaches, so he fired the coach, his staff, and the star player. How long do you think it would take for the championship coach and the star player to get another job? About a nanosecond! Why? Because they were winners and had created a reputation for winning.

This is not such a far-fetched scenario for the uncertain, volatile times we are experiencing. Sports teams often get dismantled and start rebuilding programs; and the players with a reputation for excellence tend to quickly get snapped up by other teams. Some years ago the owner of the Chicago Bulls decided the players and coach were getting older, and he needed to prepare for the future. So he decided to disband the team and start all over and draft a group of younger players. Once the word got out, it was just hours before the coach, Phil Jackson, the coach who had led them to six championships, was picked up by another team. And many of the players, even though they were older, were picked up by other teams quickly as well.

You might not be a sports figure, but take a moment to imagine yourself being the type of person who is winning on a daily basis, who is creating a reputation for excellence. In doing so, you are creating a demand for your services! If this dream is realized, you, too, will have a reputation where people want you on their team.

Choosing Excellence Is Not Always the Easy Choice

I must share that having an attitude of excellence can be challenging and seen as a threat to those who don't have it. My son is an attorney and on his first job out of law school he was hired as a temporary project employee. He was hired to do a specific project, which was estimated to take four weeks. He went in for his first day on the job and came home that evening and said he needed to talk to me. He said he was confused because I always told him to be excellent in every job you do, and do the absolute best you can in doing that job! He shared that when he got to the job all the other workers gave him different advice than me. They told him to slow his work pace and see if he could stretch this four-week job out for eight or twelve weeks. If a task should take a day, to see if he could find a way to have it take three or four days. They said, "Don't work too hard, because if you do you will work yourself out of a job!"

My son asked me what he should do, and I quickly told him, "Do exactly what I told you to do! Be excellent! If you can, see if you can do the work in three and a half weeks with the same level of excellence! Work hard, because you are developing your personal brand and reputation, and it should be a reputation for excellence, not dragging your feet! If they pay you a dollar, give them two dollars' worth of work. If they want you there at 9 AM, see if you can get there by 8:45 and stay until 5:15 or 5:30 and get more done. Create a reputation of excellence! It will pay great dividends over time and pave a path for you in the future!"

My son did as I recommended. He got there early, would often work through lunch, and stay later after everyone else had left, and he was able to complete the project in three and a half weeks. The other workers told him he was stupid, because he had worked himself out of a job. Yet, about a week later my son got a call from the office of the director of the program, who said that they had been watching him and had seen his work ethic. And they were calling to offer him a position as the director of the office where he had worked, at double the salary! Excellence always pays the best dividends.

How to Be Great

When I first started my speaking career I spoke to young people at schools around America and gave a speech called "How to Be Great!" I didn't consider myself to be great, but I had studied great people and was passing on the knowledge I'd gained from observing those great people. In retrospect, I realize those lessons became a foundation for my life and the foundation for this book! I will share many of those principles throughout this book. So, what does greatness really mean?

Greatness is a level of accomplishment that every business, church, for-profit or nonprofit organization, and every success-minded person aspires to achieve. It is a word that is both captivating and compelling. Greatness by its pure definition means to be *outstanding, exceptional, remarkable, and extraordinary*—that which is extra and beyond ordinary. My question to you is, do you want to reach a level where you are considered to have achieved greatness? Are you a success-minded person aspiring to reach that level that is outstanding, exceptional, remarkable, and extraordinary?

So, if you know you want to reach that elite status, the question then is, how do you do it? My answer to that question is that greatness is achieved by adopting a new attitude, an attitude of excellence!

That brings us to this question: What does excellence really mean? Webster's dictionary defines *excellence* as that which is "of the best and finest quality; that which is superior, outstanding, and first class." It is going the extra mile and going beyond the call of duty. Therefore, excellence is a quality that is to be modeled. I contend that excellence is not only a quality, but also an attitude! It is an attitude that makes you want to do more, be more, and achieve more.

Vince Lombardi, the great football coach who took a team that was a perennial loser to three consecutive NFL championships and victories in the first two Super Bowls, said, "Perfection is not attainable, but if we chase perfection, we can catch excellence!" The desire for greatness, for achievement, for excellence, directs your actions. In this way, the pursuit of excellence becomes a habit. Aristotle acknowledged this. He said, "We are what we repeatedly do. Excellence, then, is not an act, but a habit."

I want to help you make excellence a habit rather than a once-in-a-while occurrence. And through this habitual pursuit, you can achieve greatness along the way!

This leads us to the word *achievement*, which is critically important in the quest for excellence. Achievement denotes that you have reached a higher level of success by not just thinking or talking about a goal but by actually doing something to accomplish the goal. And then when you take it to the next level by actually doing and *being excellent* at the task, then you are really cooking with gas. Simply put, achievement takes work! Some success can be the result of luck, such as hitting the lottery, but achievement always involves work—which means specific effort, action, initiative, and working diligently to accomplish the goal! And doing excellent work means that you have not only put in the work, but you also have done it at a level where you stand out from the crowd.

Basketball great Michael Jordan didn't make his high school's varsity basketball team the first time he tried out. But that didn't stop him from pursuing his dream to play. He continued to work on his dream and went on to become one of the greatest basketball players of all time. He once said, "Talent is God given, but ability and achievement take work!" And I again add to that statement that being excellent takes consistent, determined work and extreme effort.

My goal with this book is to help you achieve more in your personal and professional pursuits and to help you reach higher in your level of excellence!

It Starts with Your Thinking

When I started my speaking career I wasn't very good. I stumbled and bumbled my way through the early presentations I gave. I realized if I wanted to be a great speaker, I needed to start with getting better, and being diligent in getting better. And I learned that it started on working on my mindset. I went to seminars and listened to audios and videos on how to think bigger, better, and greater. I needed to not only think better thoughts, but also I needed to act in a better way. During that growth time for my personal development, I was reminded of the lessons I had learned from my parents, who always stressed excellence and a strong work ethic. They emphasized that those two items could transform my life. It was only when I got older that I realized they were simply sharing great biblical principles to help me to achieve great success in my future.

Scripture teaches us that transformation always starts with thinking. "Do not be conformed to this world, but be transformed by the renewal of your mind . . ." (Romans 12:2). Scripture also teaches us to be diligent in what we do within our work. "A slack hand causes poverty, but the hand of the diligent makes rich" (Proverbs 10:4).

Being excellent always starts with our thinking. We need to think big and to be diligent in our actions. What is your thinking, your mindset, your attitude?

Accentuate the Positive, Eliminate the Negative

I mentioned in the preface how former Ford CEO Alan Mulally focused on the power of staying positive. I have witnessed this trait in many other great leaders as well. I have seen how these successful men and women dream big and believe that their dreams are possible. They feel good about themselves. They have a positive, confident self-esteem and positive expectations for the future. When I used to give my "How to Be Great" speech, where I shared with the audience some of the things I'd learned from studying great people, I would talk about the power of positivity and how to develop it. The more I learned, the more I used the principles and the more I discovered that the principles work. I would recommend that people read and listen to something positive daily. I also recommended that they express positive affirmations to themselves daily in order to generate positive self-esteem. I would tell them that if no one else encouraged them, then they needed to encourage themselves. They could do this by speaking to themselves as they go throughout their day or by looking in a mirror and telling themselves that they can and will achieve their goals. I encourage you to do this as well.

I also recommended that people make a commitment to stay away from negative people. It is critical to stay away from small-minded, itty-bitty, petty-thinking people. People who tell you what you can't do rather than what you can do; people who discourage rather than encourage. Those people are the ones who suffer from "possibility blindness," which means they cannot see the possibilities for themselves and assume that it also will not be possible for anyone else to achieve their goals. So when I spoke about being great, I would encourage the audience to hold on to their positive vision by making it a point to stay away from negative people. I encourage you to do the same. Make a point to only hang around those who support you and your goal for excellence in your life.

A third characteristic of great people I've observed, which is connected to positivity, is how the great ones don't buy into fear, and don't accept false paradigms that most other people accept as true. For example, when I spoke to young people, their struggle was often accepting the false paradigm that where they come from determines where they will end up and believing the lie that being smart is being a nerd. When I spoke with adults, their issue was believing that their past determined their future. They let themselves accept the thought that they were not good enough, and that their past failures dictated their future successes or lack thereof. That is a false paradigm! Another false paradigm is believing that your age determines your success or possibilities. Age does not determine your success, unless you allow it to limit your possibilities. Just like I told those listening to my speech, you need to know the truth, which is that anyone, young or old, can achieve greatness, even if they start with failure or mediocre success. Your past does not determine your future!

Do not give into your doubts. William Shakespeare said, "Our doubts are traitors, and make us lose the good we oft might win, by fearing to attempt."

In my book *It Only Takes a Minute to Change Your Life,* I share the failures of Abraham Lincoln before he became president, and how he refused to let his past failures determine his future success. This is the story of a man who failed in business at the age of 21, was defeated in a legislative race at age 22, failed again in business at age 24, and lost his sweetheart at age 26 when she died of typhoid. He had a nervous breakdown at age 27, lost a congressional race at age 34 and another one at 36, lost a senatorial race at age 45, failed in his effort to become vice president at age 47, and lost another senatorial race at age 49. Then, at age 52, he was elected president of the United States!

So don't be afraid to fail. In fact, look forward to failure, because if you fail and learn from your failure you are essentially closer to your goal. Believing the truth and being positive in our thoughts, words, and actions is all part of having the right mindset. Also, when you stay positive about your possibilities, it makes it easier to stay persistent, which is a necessary trait to have in your quest for excellence.

Mindset Before Skillset

Let me give you an example of the importance of mindset from a blog I wrote that features a lesson from my friend Delatorro McNeal. Delatorro is someone who articulated the critical impact of mindset on success. Here is an excerpt from a blog post I wrote about him and the importance of positioning for mindset and skillset:

> My friend Delatorro McNeal II is one of America's great speakers and peak performance trainers. He teaches audiences around the world about the importance of developing your mindset to achieve peak performance. I met Delatorro when he was working on his graduate studies at the University of Central Florida. He told me he wanted to be a speaker, and I told him the steps he needed to take in order to grow a speaking business.

Delatorro not only did what I recommended, but he also did everything with a spirit of excellence. He consistently went the extra mile.

Delatorro went on to become one of America's top keynote speakers and peak performance experts. He invited me to attend a seminar he was conducting in the DC area and during his speech he shared an illustration about mindset and skillset that I felt was one of the best I had heard. He shared that many people are looking for the secret to success, the single silver bullet, the single key that will unlock the padlock to success. Yet, he went on to share that there is no single key to unlock the padlock. Delatorro shared that in reality, success is not a single key, but a combination lock!

Delatorro shared that success is the result of numerous concepts that will be necessary to unlock the combination. Then after you discover the numerous concepts that will unlock the combination lock, you then need to know their correct sequence. If the concepts are not in the right order, you will not be able to unlock your success.

Delatorro gave me the clinical reason why I focused so strongly on mindset first and then skillset. I knew it was important to have both mindset development and skillset development, but it was also critical that you work on your mindset first, then work on skillset. Why? If you put the skillset before your mindset development, you might get some short-term success, but it typically won't last.

I have found that the situation is best seen in professional sports. Every year on draft day in the National Football League or National Basketball Association we see a new set of young athletes who are drafted into the professional ranks and become millionaires. I applaud their accomplishment every year and hope that they will have great success, both personally and professionally. The challenge is that statistics show that over 60 percent of professional athletes are broke five years after retirement. The reason is because most have worked on a skillset before working on a mindset. Yet, those who work on their mindset, then work on their skillsets are those who expand beyond the original skillset and unlock the padlock to long-term success. They are able to add additional income streams to their wealth after their playing days are over, such as commentating or becoming successful entrepreneurs or becoming team owners. So it is critical to long-term success to work on mindset and skillset, but to do it in the right order.

This book is designed to do just that: work first on attitude development (mindset/attitude) and then work on skillset development (excellence), so you, too, can continue to have long-term success. Through this book I want to help you develop a new framework for winning more, by achieving excellence. This framework, built on these two powerful principles of attitude and excellence, is a new way of building your future by focusing on personal and professional development, a new way of building the attitude muscle and the mindset of excellence for both an organization and the individuals who work in that organization. I believe wholeheartedly that the best way to grow any organization is to grow the people in the organization. And the best way to grow your individual future is to grow yourself! If you move forward with this mindset, and you add a commitment to excellence, you will achieve greatness!

When you have a mindset of excellence, you learn that you win each and every time you do what you do, even when the box score doesn't represent a win, because you create a reputation for the constant and never-ending pursuit of excellence. My goal is for you to prosper and do more in the future than you've done in the past. In short, I want to help you create a more fulfilling future while making more money, and making a greater difference—starting right now!

The Pursuit of Better

So what is the will to win all about? Well, as I noted earlier, attitude is the why you do what you do, and excellence is the how you do what you do. Great organizations do what they do because *they want to win*! They have the mindset that they are going to be the best of the best and take the actions to achieve that goal. So an organization's journey to five-star success starts with attitude, with mindset—then it takes action and does all it can to get there. A case in point is the Four Seasons Hotel in Washington, DC.

When Christopher Hunsberger was the general manager at the Four Seasons Hotel in Washington, DC, he developed a new culture of excellence and a concept called "Better!" I read about Mr. Hunsberger after the Washington, DC, Four Seasons was named one of "America's Best Hotels" in *USA Today* and designated a Five-Star Hotel by the Mobil Five-Star Hotel Committee, a rating of distinction within the hospitality industry. I interviewed Mr. Hunsberger, and he shared some powerful insights with me about how his hotel climbed from a very good hotel to one of America's best.

When Mr. Hunsberger became the general manager of the Four Seasons, it was a very nice four-star hotel, yet he dreamed of creating a world-class, five-star hotel. The Four Seasons was well regarded in the hospitality industry, but it did not have the distinctive Mobil Five-Star rating. The previous management had tried and tried but had been unable to achieve the five-star rating. Mr. Hunsberger came into the position with his eyes wide open and knew it would be difficult and challenging, yet he believed it was possible. He set out on a plan to make that dream a reality.

He started by selling his staff on his vision of creating a five-star hotel. It was going to take a committed team effort to achieve the goal, and he knew he had to sell everyone in the organization, from the top to the bottom, on this goal. The next step was a major transformation of the physical structure. The

Four Seasons underwent a $25 million renovation, resulting in a beautiful facility. Once the renovation of the building was complete, he gathered his staff and asked, "Isn't this a gorgeous renovation? Isn't it exceptional? Now what can we do to transform our service to parallel the new look of the hotel? What can we do to create a service culture beyond compare?" He knew that once the building was renovated, he had to start working on the thinking of his team. He had to renovate the thinking of the team so they, too, could be exceptional.

Mr. Hunsberger knew that other hotel chains could easily replicate the physical improvements simply by spending money. Many hotels have fancy marble in their lobbies and luxurious rooms, but the difference between the good hotels and the great hotels is always the service. Great hotels consistently "wow" the customers with their service.

Mr. Hunsberger told me that he went to each department and asked the associates, "What can you do on a daily basis to improve service so we can create a hotel beyond compare?" He encouraged them to get excited about developing new ideas, and he reminded them that one of their goals was to get the customers so amazed by the service that they would tell everyone they knew about their experience at the Four Seasons Hotel.

Together, they created a concept called "Better!" which focused on "Being Better and Doing Better" each and every day. The goal was to create an intuitive service culture that allowed associates to anticipate the needs of the customers, instead of waiting to be asked. He said the title and concept of Better! was built on the little poem his grandmother had taught him as a child: "Good, better, best, never let it rest! Until your good is better, and your better is best!"

Mr. Hunsberger and his team continued to work on their goal to achieve Mobil's elusive five-star rating. Each year they tried to achieve it and continued to improve but did not receive the five-star award. Even when they didn't make it, they made a commitment that they would keep working on achieving and improving. They created a slogan that they chanted every day: "Five-star or bust, five-star or bust." And they kept getting better.

After five years of working on the dream of five-star status, they finally achieved the goal and were awarded the Five-Star rating. They were written up in national newspapers and industry magazines as "One of the best, of the best, in the world!" They were proclaimed "America's Newest Five-Star Success Story."

Yet they realized their achievement was not in hitting the goal as much as it was in the culture they had developed in the process. They had created an attitude of excellence and a culture of Better! The culture of Better! was ingrained in the minds of the staff, and even though they have now been awarded the five-star status for more than a dozen consecutive years, they continue to find new ways to amaze their customers, each and every day.

This Four Seasons success story shows the impact of having a focus of excellence. Do you know what you're shooting for? Motivational speaker Zig Ziglar had many famous sayings. One of them was this: "If you aim at nothing, you will hit it every time." We must focus. Five-star organizations aim at something very specific: being the best at what they do. They have a will to win. We must have this will to win inside us as well.

• • •

So, let's go! Let's get going in our quest to achieve greatness with an attitude of excellence! As you read about the five secrets to five-star success in part one and the five steps to personal transformation in part two, think about ways you can implement these things into your life. I will offer some suggestions and encouragement along the way. Also, be sure to keep the goal of excellence in mind. Remember, it starts with the will to win!

The Five Secrets of Creating a Five-Star Culture of Excellence

Implement Dynamic Leadership Development

Develop Leaders at Every Level of the Organization

The first ingredient in the secret sauce to five-star success is the ability to lead well, which happens through continual personal and professional development. Great organizations are leaders in their fields—they're the best of the best—and they always look to have leaders throughout the ranks. These leaders could be the managers, middle managers, or line workers; they could be those who upload programs on the web, answer phones, or clean the buildings. Whatever their role, these are employees who are empowered to do whatever is necessary to provide excellent service to customers.

Great organizations know that their power is in their people. They recognize that although technological upgrades are important, the major difference between good organizations and great organizations is always the people who work in those organizations. Simply put, great organizations have great people.

Investing in Their People

In order to have good leaders at every level of the organization, great companies develop their people. Of course, before they develop them, they start with the best! This is often overlooked in how organizations attain success, but it's a key factor. The best companies always commit to getting the best people. Just as great sports teams are always trying to get the best players, so, too, do great organizations because great leaders know that great people are the secret to creating outstanding organizations.

But if they can't hire them or acquire them, then like sports teams, they do the next best thing: take the ones they have and make the commitment to make them better. Case in point: I was asked to be the closing speaker for a Dell Computer international leadership conference. I went a day early to hear some of the other presenters they had invited—they had some real heavy hitters I wanted to hear. The night before my speech, I had dinner with the program director. I mentioned to him that I was amazed at the program they had put together and honored to be in the mix of speakers. I did have one question for him, though. I was intrigued as to why they would spend such a great amount of money on this meeting. I wondered why they would make such a major investment for such a small group of people, only three hundred or so of their top managers.

In response, he shared a powerful tenet of success. He said, "We want to be the best in the world at what we do. We want to lead the field. And in order to be the best, we must have the best people; and, if we cannot *hire* them, we will *make* them!"

I said, "Wow!" For me that was a real "aha" moment, because it brought to the surface one of the best-kept secrets of super-successful companies. Five-star companies always look to have the best people to work for them and are constantly looking to hire, acquire, or develop them. If they cannot hire them, they will work to make them better. It is like a wise chef who looks to get the best raw materials and turn them into fabulous dishes. Or like jewelers who look for the best raw diamonds to make beautiful jewelry. They are making a commitment to get the best in order to develop or create something amazing.

Great organizations know they not only need to have the best people in order to achieve the best results but also that they must grow their people in order to grow their productivity and profits. They know that there is a direct correlation between the success of their employees and the success of the organization. So these organizations consistently invest in the growth and development of their workforce.

In fact, according to *Forbes* magazine, American companies spend $70 billion a year on training and developing their employees. This amount has been increasing each year for the past several years. An Association for Talent Development 2016 study sponsored by LinkedIn and Study.com showed that organizations spent an average $1,273 per employee on training, with employees in training for a total of nearly one workweek (34.1 hours). Of this, the largest percentage of employee training was on managerial and supervisory skills.

Michael Mankins, a partner with leadership consulting firm Bain & Company, noted in an article in *Fast Company* that only 15 percent of employees at most companies are star players, and that it's only 1 percent more at companies like Apple, Google, and Dell. So while companies strive to get the best, they still must invest in developing their employees. *Forbes* contributor and Deloitte consultant Josh Bersin says companies tell him it takes three to five years "to take a seasoned professional and make them fully productive."

Happy, Engaged Employees Have an Impact on Profits

Five-star organizations train and develop their employees so they have the skills they need to do the best job they can. But great organizations don't want just capable employees; they want happy, industrious employees. They know that having happy employees affects the level of service offered to customers, which in turns affects the bottom line.

It is critical to understand the impact that happy people have on great service. Studies show that if people are happy, they tend to give better service. This applies to an employee's happiness at work as well as home. An article in *USA Today* cited studies showing that people who have happier home lives tend to perform better at work. So being happy with both your job and your home life can have a profound impact on your effectiveness at work. This is why great service organizations make it a part of their service to continually check on the happiness of their employees.

Richard Hadden and Bill Catlette state this concept wonderfully in their popular book *Contented Cows Give Better Milk*. They say that those who are happy at home tend to be happier at work and are exponentially more productive than those who aren't happy at home. Therefore, those who have a higher level of internal satisfaction both at home and at work tend to give better service to customers and enjoy better employee relations. Those who have drama at home often bring that drama to work and it passes on to how they treat the customer.

Richard and Bill are absolutely correct: Happy people, like happy cows, tend to give better output and create better results and greater profits for the company. I encourage everyone to work on being happier in their day-to-day lives (which is why I have added the second half of this book for everyone to enjoy and learn from).

So, we see that happy employees lead to better profits. But what are the ways that organizations use to make their employees happier? In preparing for a program for the Society of Human Resource Managers (SHRM), I had the opportunity to interview a number of top corporate leaders from around the world. I asked them, "What are the secrets to your creating happy and productive employees?" The information I received was priceless.

Encourage Your People

To create happy and productive employees, the first thing great organizations do is encourage their employees. The leaders at the SHRM program told me that the more employees are encouraged to do their best, the more morale went up and the more productivity went up. As employees were empowered to communicate honestly and openly, their performance improved. Also, those companies that find or develop good talent are more often willing to work with them to keep them engaged, even if the employees' lives change and they have to relocate to other cities.

Keep Your People Engaged

The second thing top-tier organizations do to create happy and productive employees is keep them engaged at work. They don't want their employees to mentally quit the job. My friend Stan Robbins, a human resources executive, shared a powerful idea about the impact of engagement, or lack thereof. Stan said, "It is bad when a person on your team quits and leaves, but it is worse when a person quits and stays. They are there in body but not engaged."

I also like to share this little thought. I was asked once, "What happens if you invest in an employee and they leave?" My answer was, "What happens if you don't invest in them and they stay?" Ouch! I recommend you invest in yourself *and* invest in your team . . . It always pays the best dividends!

Al Cornish, the Chief Learning Officer of Norton Healthcare, said:

> In today's corporate climate, organizations are looking for strategies and ways to *improve overall employee engagement.* Employment is up, but engagement is down. The struggle is how does an organization get the "best" and "maximum" performance out of a new workforce, which includes the millennial generation. To create a high-performing team, you need all employees pulling in the same direction. We realize that attitude is *fundamental and foundational* to an employee's engagement and performance.

Many of the managers I interviewed said they looked for new and creative ways to keep people on their teams engaged and excited about their jobs, even if they lived in different cities. One noted, "Everyone has bumps in their lives. If you are able to unshackle your mind and think differently, you are able to open up incredible possibilities for engagement, productivity, and growth of the person and the company."

Organizations that are willing to think and act differently so they stay engaged are not only strengthening their bottom line, they are creating employees who can become the organizations' best marketing vehicles for adding great new talent. Happy and excited team members are more apt to tell friends and become magnets for attracting high-quality people to join the company. To get the best people, top organizations know that *they must be willing to think differently and empower their people to do the same.*

Coach Your Team to Have an Attitude of Excellence

In a special Super Bowl edition of *Parade* magazine in 2008, Jeremy Schaap wrote an article about Super Bowl history, with a specific emphasis on how Vince Lombardi changed a losing group of football players in Green Bay, Wisconsin, into a team that became legendary. Vince Lombardi was a football coach who took over a tattered team in Green Bay, Wisconsin, called the Green Bay Packers. His name became synonymous with winning and excellence. Upon his death in 1970 the NFL Super Bowl trophy was named in his honor. Vince Lombardi is an example of a person who used a positive attitude and a commitment to excellence to change the destiny of an organization and an entire sports league!

The article shares some comments from Bart Starr, who was the quarterback of the team when they had won only one game the season before Lombardi became their coach. Starr describes the first time he met Vince Lombardi. It was the first team meeting with the new coach, and Vince Lombardi told the team,

"Gentlemen, I want you to know that we are going to relentlessly chase perfection, knowing full well we will not catch it, because nothing is perfect. But we are going to relentlessly chase it, because in the process we will cross a street called excellence, and in doing that we will catch excellence!" They did, in fact, create excellence and went on to win five league championships (including three in a row) and the first two Super Bowls.

Bart Starr said that after that first meeting with Lombardi, he ran to a phone and called his wife and told her that something was different and that something had changed! He told his wife that the team was going to win, and win big, because the new coach has convinced him they could, and they would, be excellent!

Bart Starr went on to be inducted into the Hall of Fame and to become a very successful businessman and philanthropist. He said that Lombardi taught him that when you "catch excellence"—the attitude of excellence—then you will be transformed and amazed at what you will accomplish, not just at work but in every part of your life.

Once while waiting at a terminal gate for a departing flight, I noticed a gentleman wearing a Green Bay Packers sweater. I recognized the gentleman from television and realized it was Paul Hornung, the star running back of the Green Bay Packers during the time of Vince Lombardi. I asked him if the stories of Vince Lombardi and how he helped the team catch the attitude of excellence were true or just urban myths. Without hesitation, he said, "Yes! Those stories are absolutely true; they are not myths! He instilled an attitude of excellence and that was the reason why we won!"

A winning team tends to be a happy team. And if organizations want to win more, they instill an attitude of excellence in their people.

When I interviewed Bill Marriott, the executive chairman of Marriott hotels, on my Sirius XM radio show and for my Wealthy Ways podcast, he told me that the people who work at Marriott are what make Marriott stand out. The associates are encouraged to show their attitude of excellence to each and every customer, each and every day, in every way they can. In fact, because Marriott recognizes that those who work for the hotel are partners in making the company successful, the organization does not call them employees but rather associates.

Marriott believes that if their people are happy, then they will go the extra mile to make sure that the customers are happy. To check this correlation, the company takes two types of surveys every few months—one for customer satisfaction levels and another for associate satisfaction levels.

Marriott Hotels and Resorts is one of my clients, and they, along with another client of mine, Ritz-Carlton, continue to increase their market shares by improving the lives of the people who work there. They know that happy, excited associates tend to share that happiness and excitement with customers, and thereby tend to give better service. (Listen to the interview with Bill Marriott on my Willie Jolley Wealthy Ways podcast available on iTunes, iHeartMedia, and Stitcher.)

Let Your People Have Fun

Southwest Airlines is another example of a company thinking differently about their people. Like Marriott, Southwest believes their people are their greatest asset. Southwest sees their employees—whom they also often call associates—as their first priority. They call it an "employee-first customer service model that focuses on the fact that happy employees tend to serve customers with greater happiness."

Herb Kelleher, the founder of Southwest Airlines, said in an interview, "Anyone can buy a plane, but our people make this airline a success. It's more than providing the customer a value. It is giving them an experience. I want our customers to leave with a smile on their face and communicate that smile to everyone they talk to that day. This is the secret . . . because our competitors can all buy airplanes, it is the experience that our associates give the customers that is the hardest thing for our competitors to imitate."

The freedom to serve the customers and have fun in the process is why Southwest can get their employees to sing, tell jokes, and even climb up in the overhead bin and say "Surprise!"

when it's opened. It is the people who create the culture of the organization.

The Process of Making Diamonds

Often people miss out on living five-star lives because they live under the misconception that only a few people are leaders. They believe if you weren't born a leader, then you will never be a leader. While it is true that some leaders are born, most leaders are developed. I see leaders like diamonds—created through a process. A diamond is initially a piece of coal, an ordinary everyday piece of coal, that is separated from the group and goes through a metamorphosis that involves some change, some challenge, some adversity, and some pressure. When it has gone through all of this and it comes out of the pressure cooker, it is no longer a piece of coal, but a diamond!

The same is true for leaders. Just as diamonds are not born diamonds, neither are leaders. When a baby is born and the doctor slaps the baby on the bottom, the doctor does not say, "Put this one in the leadership group!" No! The doctor will say, "This is a beautiful baby with incredible potential, and if this baby develops that potential, then this baby can go on and do great things in the future!" The possibilities for that baby are limitless if the baby makes the decision to develop him- or herself. That baby may one day become a world-famous doctor, an award-winning educator, or a massively successful businessperson, or that baby may one day become the president of the United States. The doctor knows that you cannot tell at that age if the baby will be a great success or not. The potential and possibilities for greatness are inherent in the baby, but at the end of the day the baby's success or failure depends mainly on the choices and decisions that the baby makes as it grows into adulthood.

Russell Conwell wrote a classic book called *Acres of Diamonds* that speaks to this in a powerful way. In the book, he wrote about an African farmer who kept hearing about the wealth that was being generated in the diamond trade. He decided to sell his farm and go out and get rich in the diamond trade. He put an ad in the newspaper and advertised that he would accept the best offer. A young man came out to see the farm, and the farmer sold it to him for pennies on the dollar just so he could get on with his diamond-hunting activities. He searched and searched for diamonds for more than ten years and never found one diamond. After years of fruitlessly searching he gave up and in complete despair he threw himself off a cliff and ended his life.

Meanwhile, back at the farm, the young man who bought it for pennies on the dollar was walking across a waterbed and saw a muddy rock that glistened in the water. He picked it up, wiped off the mud, and placed it on the mantel above his fireplace. A few weeks later a friend came to visit from the big city and saw the glistening rock on the mantel. The friend from the city asked the young guy if he knew what it was. The young guy said, "Well I think it's just a pretty rock!" The friend from the city said, "No! It's a diamond, a big diamond!" The waterbed was filled with diamonds, all covered with mud. All they needed was to be wiped off and cleaned. The moral of the story is that you do not have to go looking for diamonds, because they can be in your backyard—in other words, the diamonds of your life are within you.

History has recorded many examples of people who were born into challenging situations, with the odds stacked against them. Yet they overcame the circumstances and achieved great success. In effect, they beat the odds and became diamonds. They became leaders of themselves! The potential was within them but they had to work to develop what was within them and maximize the potential.

Five-star organizations understand this concept. That is why they invest in their people. Leaders at every level of the organization who think and work like a team inspire greater performance, productivity, and profits. Leaders focus on developing their people by improving their attitude, their aptitude, and their appetite. Leaders know that a winning attitude and a decision to develop an aptitude, or skillset, based on excellence, followed by a strong drive to reach excellence, is the trifecta for winning teams.

We have learned that one of the keys to leadership development is to grasp the concept that it does not matter where you come from; it only matters where you are going! I encourage you to develop the leader within you, and if you do, and continue to do so, you will definitely be on your way to greatness.

Investing in Yourself

In order to have five-star success, organizations need leaders at every level. From entry-level employees to managers to middle managers, all should be developing into leaders who are proactive and forward thinkers. But before you can lead many, you must be able to lead one: yourself! To become a leader, you must stand up on the inside and make the commitment to get better and continue to make that commitment on a daily basis.

Leadership development is a critical step in the five-star success formula. What can you learn from this first secret of how five-star organizations create a culture of excellence? Are you serious about success? Are you willing to work on yourself and become better? Are you willing to make a commitment to lifelong learning? Are you willing to stand up and be a leader? The old saying states, "If you don't have something you are willing to stand up for, you will fall for anything!" We must make a commitment to become more effective leaders. It is critical at five-star organizations that everyone on their teams becomes "a leader of one."

Lifelong Learning

I firmly believe that there is a leader in everyone—but you have to develop yourself. Unfortunately, statistics show that although most people want greater results in life, they are not willing to continue to work on themselves. Statistics show that the average person will not read any more informational or self-help books after they finish school. Most people will look at television for hours and never read a book or listen to an educational audio program. Will you be like most people or will you stand out?

My friend Charlie "Tremendous" Jones was one of the legends in the self-development arena and was often heard saying, "In five years you will be the same person you are today except for the people you meet and the books you read!" Who are the people you're meeting? What are you reading?

I love the concept about lifelong learning that is gleaned from the following statement and question: "If you ever go to a ten-million-dollar home, it will always have a library. The question is, does the person who buys that ten-million-dollar home buy it because it has a library or does their library allow them to buy it?"

Benjamin Franklin, the great statesman and inventor, said, "If you take a coin from your purse and invest it in your mind, in time it will come pouring out of your mind and overflow your purse!" I like to say it like this: "The greatest investment you can ever make is the one you make in yourself, because the pennies you invest in your thinking will produce dollars you can place in your wallet!"

So, what are you reading? What are you listening to? What skillsets are you developing? How are you trying to get better? What are you doing to become a better leader? You must take responsibility for your success and make a commitment to work on yourself and become better! If you do this, you will get closer to living your five-star life, which leads to you being a valuable part of a five-star organization.

I am so glad you are reading this book, because it qualifies you as one of the rare ones. Just by picking up this book, you have made a step that the average person will never make.

Ownership Mentality

I recently saw a report that noted that the greatest success stories within organizations involve those people who decided to think like leaders and also decided to think and act like they had some stake in the actual success of the organization. They decided to imagine that they were part owners, and acted in accordance with that thinking. They realized that owners work at a different level from their employees. The interesting thing is that many of the people I know who have achieved massive success are those who were once employees but thought like owners and eventually became owners—all because they developed ownership thinking.

I encourage you to imagine yourself as an owner, a leader. Think of yourself as a powerful part of the organization, and then think how you should act when you are in that position. Once you imagine it, then act like you are in that position. If you change your thinking and change how you act, often you will change the results that you are able to generate. You will be amazed at the new results and the impact they have on your success and the success of the organization!

See Change as an Ally

Don't Just Go Through
Change, Grow Through It

What are your thoughts about change? Do you see it as an enemy, something to be resisted at all costs, or do you welcome it? And how do you handle change? Do you simply endure changes in your life or organization, or do you learn from them?

Imagine change as a supersonic freight train, speeding down the track toward us. This train is constantly moving in our direction, in one form or another. Due to technology, change is coming more rapidly each and every day. For example, the new "top of the line" smartphone I bought a couple years ago was said to be the fastest and most efficient at that time, but a couple years later I was informed by a techie friend that my phone was just about obsolete. We laughed and he recommended I simply buy a newer, faster model! Technology is making change happen even more rapidly.

So, it's a fact of life: Change is inevitable, whether we like it or not. We cannot stop it from happening, we cannot stop it from coming our way, but we can choose how we respond to it.

What's Your Response to Change?

There are several ways we can respond to change. Option one is to stand in front of the train, cross our arms, and say, "I don't want to change. I've made up my mind that I'm not moving! I have always done business this way and it works fine for me." This is not a good option because the train will run you over! Option two is to step back and ignore it, or sit and watch it pass you by while saying, "Isn't that a pretty train!" You might say, "I'm not sure about that internet. I let my kids play on it. I check my emails maybe once a week." Again, not a good choice because the train will pass you by. I recommend option three.

Option three is to fully embrace it. When the change train comes your way, get on board and ride it. And if you are really wise, you will not only ride it, but you also will find a way to drive it. Jack Welch, the former CEO of General Electric (GE), who was often called the "CEO of the Century," was known to say, "Only those who drive change maximize their potential and possibilities!"

Imagine this scenario. A young man who had recently dropped out of college sees the change train coming his way, so he jumps on board. He rides the change train for a short time and then makes his way up to the front of the train. He sees an older gentleman driving the change train and asks if he could drive it for a few minutes. Initially the older gentleman says no, but the young man is persistent and keeps asking and asking until the older gentleman gives in with the stipulation that it can only be for a few minutes.

The young man takes the wheel of the change train and starts driving it. After a few minutes the older gentleman taps the young man on the shoulder and says the time for the test drive is over. But the young man says he wants to keep driving the change train, and fights to keep driving. We know him today as a man who continues to drive the change train. His name is Bill Gates, one of the wealthiest people in the world. He proves that Jack Welch was right—only those who drive change maximize their potential and possibilities!

It's been said, "It is best to ride a horse in the direction it is going," but I say that you should get on board and ride the change train in the direction it is going, because the change train is coming your way.

Remember, you always have the power of choice in terms of your response to change. You can resist it, you can ignore it, or you can get on board and ride it. Change is inevitable, but your response is optional. If you are going to have five-star success, then you must be willing to change and see change not as an enemy but as an ally.

Change's Role in Success

Change is a part of life and a major part of any successful journey. Some years ago I was speaking in Fayetteville, North Carolina, the home of the Fort Bragg military base. The driver of the car service that picked me up had been a military man. I asked him how long he had been driving and he responded, "Just a short while." He explained that he had made a career in the army—until they let him go!

"Are you telling me that you were downsized from the army?" I asked. "Yes," he said and proceeded to give me the details. Initially, he been very puzzled—until he had a conversation with one of his friends, who asked about the circumstance that led to his dismissal. He told the friend, "I've been in the service about twenty-six years and I've done the same job well and consistently all twenty-six years." The friend asked, "So are you saying you have been doing the same job, the same way, for the last twenty-six years, and you didn't work on getting better? If that is the case, you needed to be fired. You didn't change, and the world and environment around you did!"

His friend helped him understand that unless you are growing and changing and trying to get better, you are at a disadvantage and are losing your value. In today's workforce no one can guarantee that you will be doing the same job in the same way tomorrow as you are doing it today. In fact, to go through twenty-six years and do the same job, the same way, is like a person who today rides around in a Gremlin car (built from 1970–78), wearing a polyester leisure suit (popular in the 1960s and 1970s), and using a typewriter rather than using a computer. As one friend said to me, "If you are not growing, then you are just taking up space!"

To thrive and survive in this changing marketplace, you must expand or become expendable. Some say you must either *grow* or *go*! Bill Freeman, the former president of Verizon Communications, told me that he was always encouraging his people to grow. He also said, "If my people are not in demand outside the organization and have no value outside the organization, they have no value on the inside of the organization!"

I am often asked about the title of my first book, *It Only Takes a Minute to Change Your Life*. People would ask me if the statement is really true—that it only takes a minute to change your life. My answer is, "Absolutely!" The minute you make a decision and move in a new direction is the minute you change your life. You might not reach your destination in a minute, but you can certainly change your direction. And when you make the decision to change and take action, you change your life!

As we move along the path to success, we are going to experience change. How we handle that change matters. *It Only Takes a Minute to Change Your Life* is a book filled with one-minute messages written to help people digest change in bite-size pieces.

Someone put it perfectly when they said, "All progress is the result of changes, yet all change is not progress!"

Creatures of Habit: Is It Change . . . or Is It You?

We all have some initial discomfort with change because we are creatures of habit. We tend to do what we always do because that is human nature. Yet, we can mold our minds to see change from a different perspective. My mother used to say something to me that helped me better understand, and change my perspective regarding the issue of change. She would say, "Willie, if you keep doing what you have been doing, you are going to keep getting what you have been getting!" (After I got enough spankings, I finally figured it out. I needed to change!)

Statistics show that most people who go to a restaurant a second time will get the exact same meal they got the first time. Most people who go to a church, synagogue, mosque, or worship center tend to sit in the same area they sat in last time they were there—and don't you dare sit in their seats, or you might see them lose their religion. If you go to a gym, you probably have a certain locker that you like to use. And if someone is using it, you may get a little out of sorts. When you put on your pants, you tend to always put the same leg in the trousers first.

We are all creatures of habit and we tend to do what we've always done, because that is the way we have always done it. Yet if you want different results, you must be willing to change. A popular definition of insanity is doing the same thing, the same way, and expecting different results. In order to win in life, we must change; and if we don't change, we lose, because we don't grow!

People *Can* Change

Years ago Heavyweight Boxing Champion Muhammad Ali was being interviewed by Howard Cosell, the noted sports announcer. Ali was preparing to go back into the ring after being away from boxing for a number of years, and Cosell mentioned that Ali was about to fight a very imposing adversary, George Foreman. This would be a championship fight and Foreman was unbeaten. Cosell asked Ali, "Muhammad, this is going to be a tough fight. Are you the same fighter you were twenty years ago when you first started fighting?"

Ali looked right at Cosell and said, "I certainly hope not! Anyone who is the same person twenty years later than they were twenty years earlier is a pitiful person!" Ali was not the same fighter. He had changed his skills, for his experience had changed. Ali took on Foreman and implemented a unique technique called the "rope-a-dope," where he leaned on the ropes and let Foreman wear himself out. Once Foreman had grown tired, Ali attacked and won the fight! Ali won the World Championship boxing title because he used change as an ally, not an enemy.

One interesting side note about that story and the power of change is that George Foreman also changed. He went from being a big, sulking, angry fighter who was mean and uncommunicative, to a pleasant, funny, and personable media personality. He has become one of America's most popular endorsement personalities and the pitchman for the famous George Foreman Grill. Plus, he went back in the ring and became the oldest man ever to win a heavyweight championship. He became a preacher, an author, a TV personality, and a big teddy bear of a man. He reinvented himself and maximized his potential by learning to see change as an ally, not an enemy!

Change and Challenge Go Hand and Hand

Typically, wherever there is change there will also be challenge. While challenge is uncomfortable, it can also be the catalyst for major growth and development and can ultimately be a key to our success. In the book *Who Moved My Cheese?* written by Dr. Spencer Johnson, there is a parable that highlights how people are so unwilling to change that they end up starving, while those who are willing to change are those who embrace change and are those who succeed and prosper.

My own story details how challenge can help you find your own success. For many years I was a nightclub singer. I sang jingles during the day and performed in nightclubs in the evenings, where I made the majority of my income. I created a nightclub act that became one of the hottest acts in the Washington, DC, area. I was awarded the Washington Area Music Association WAMMIE (the Washington, DC, version of a Grammy Award) three years in a row for best jazz singer and best entertainer (to enjoy some of my jazz music, go to www. williejolley.com/jazz). Most weekends, my show had sold-out performances and people had to make reservations weeks in advance. I was making money and having lots of fun.

One night after arriving at the nightclub, the club manager told me he wanted to talk to me after the show. I was excited. We had been selling out for months and had made them a lot of money, so I was looking forward to a raise. I told the guys in the band, "Hey, they finally want to talk! We're finally going to get our raise!"

I walked into the club manager's office that evening, and he said, "Willie, you were great tonight! The people loved you! You know we have made a lot of money since you have been performing here."

I was getting more and more excited by the minute. With each word he spoke I saw dollar signs. I was ready to get to the bottom line as quickly as I could. I said, "That's great! So when do we get our raise?"

He said, "Raise? No, that's not why I asked you in. See, the owners want a better return on their investment. Now that the club is full, the only way to get a bigger return on the investment is to cut costs. And since the band is the biggest cost, we are going to make a change." They had come up with something else that was filling up nightclubs for a lot less money. They had bought a karaoke machine! I asked, "But what about my bills?" That night, I learned no one cares about your bills, except you and the people you owe!

I had been replaced by a karaoke machine and I was devastated. I had done everything that I could do to help the owners grow their business. I had done radio interviews to promote the club, sent out my own postcard mailers to invite people, and I had even made promotional appearances all over town. I did all of this for the owners, and I never asked for any money for this promotional work because I was trying to help them grow their business. Yet I still got fired, because it was cheaper to have a machine than to have a live band.

I was completely depressed and didn't know what I was going to do. It was during this low point that a friend gave me the motivational tape *The Strangest Secret* by Earl Nightingale. He shared a quote from the great African military leader Hannibal, who took elephants over the Swiss Alps, which stated, "If you cannot find a way, then you must make a way!" That struck a chord with me. I had a problem, but, more importantly, I had a decision to make. I had to decide whether I was going to keep doing things the way I had been doing them or whether I was going to change. I decided to change!

That was the beginning of a new life for me. I began to devour motivational material. I realized I needed to change what I put inside of me in order to change what came out of me—new thinking and thus new action. I wasn't sure what I was going to do, but I knew I had to start moving in a positive direction to get something done.

I took a part-time job at Montgomery County Community College in Maryland, working as a counselor for high-risk students. At the end of the semester we had an awards luncheon for the students who had stayed in school and improved their grade point averages. The director of the program asked me to speak at the luncheon about how we had accomplished the goal. While I had no real idea what I was going to say, I prepared a short speech. As I prepared my presentation, I decided to add an inspirational song at the end, like I was used to doing in my nightclub act.

On the day of the awards luncheon, I delivered my speech and sang my song. The audience gave me a standing ovation. I assumed it was for the song, but after the speech, a number of people came up and asked if they could get a copy of my notes. I was shocked! And out of that speech I received more invitations to speak.

After the semester ended, I was contacted by the District of Columbia public school system, who asked me to head up a new drug prevention program called "Positive Images." This program was designed to mix music and entertainment as a drug prevention vehicle. I took the job and started working with a group of students who were talented in music and drama to develop skits and musical performances that would project a positive image and positive reasons to stay away from drugs and violence. As a part of the job, I was invited to speak to students and staff members at schools about making wise choices. Again I added elements from my entertainment years and it became a big hit! I received more and more invitations to speak.

It was during that time I discovered something within me that I never knew existed—the ability to use words to communicate, to speak in public, as opposed to just communicating in music. I gave speeches to school kids, and from the school programs, I received invitations to speak for the teachers' association meetings. From the teachers' meetings, many would ask if I could come speak to their church groups. When I went to speak at the church events, the members would ask if I could bring my message of hope and inspiration to their jobs. There were invitations to speak from companies like Verizon, Martin Marietta, and Marriott to government agencies such as the Department of Transportation, the Social Security Administration, and the Census Bureau. Within a year, I had left my school job and started speaking full time.

Not too long after I started speaking as my full-time profession, Les Brown, the "dean of motivational speaking," heard me speak and sing. He invited me to be the opening act for

Dr. Willie Jolley with Gladys Knight, Les Brown, and Billy Preston during the Music and Motivation Dream Team Tour.

his new Music and Motivation Dream Team Tour. This tour featured Les Brown, Billy Preston, and Gladys Knight. They were looking for an opening act that combined those two elements—music and motivation—and I was it!

As a result of being on tour with Les and Gladys, I was introduced to a number of radio executives. I mentioned I had been a jingle singer and had provided one-minute commercials, so I asked if they would be interested in adopting a short radio show called "The Willie Jolley Magnificent Motivational Minute." One executive thought it was a good idea, so we recorded the one-minute shows and started airing them. They were a hit. After about a year, the motivational minute show was syndicated across the United States. From there I was invited to do a longer show on Sirius XM Radio, which grew to become one of the most popular self-help shows on the Sirius XM network.

Out of the blue one day, a book publisher called. He had been riding into work and heard me on the radio and liked my message. He wondered if I would be interested in putting some of those ideas into a book. I said I had never written a book and didn't consider myself a very good writer, so I would have to think about it. Then he started talking about money and I quickly told him, "I just thought about it!" I started writing the book that day.

That first book was *It Only Takes a Minute to Change Your Life,* mentioned above, and it quickly became a best-seller in the United States. It has gone on to be translated into numerous languages and has become a best-seller in Australia, China, Japan, India, and several African countries. My second book, *A Setback Is a Setup for a Comeback,* was released a few years later, and it too became an international best-seller and has been translated into even more languages than my first book.

Not long after, I recorded my first PBS special, called *Dare 2 Dream, Dare 2 Win*, to motivate young people to stay away from drugs, alcohol, negative people, and mediocrity. This was a live taping in a high school and it has gone on to become one of the top-selling drug prevention and violence prevention motivational DVD programs for youth in America. And it still is one of the top-selling DVDs on my website, www.williejolley.com. We have also been raising funds through my nonprofit organization, Jolley Good News (www.jolleygoodnews.org), to donate copies to schools and juvenile justice facilities across America. We believe we can dissuade those who want to create violence in schools and help create more leaders who want to positively change the world.

I continued to speak to youth and then to colleges and corporations, and a decade after starting my speaking career, I got a call from Toastmasters International, informing me that I had just been named "One of the Outstanding Five Speakers in the World" for that year. Next, I was inducted into the Speaker Hall of Fame by the National Speakers Association. A few years later, I was named "One of the 5 Leadership Speakers in America" by speaking.com, and not long after that I was named "A Legend of the Speaking Industry" by the Veterans Speakers Association. All of this occurred because I had been fired and replaced by a karaoke machine—and I had moved forward after that devastating change, willing to try something different.

What lesson did I learn? I learned that there are times when change will be thrust upon us, and that is when challenge comes into play. Change happens to us all. Change is a bend in the road we are following, but a bend in the road does not have to be the end of the road, unless we fail to change. Remember: Change is not the enemy; it is an ally! You can make it work for you rather than against you.

It's Your Choice

If you want success, you must learn to embrace the three Cs for success: change, challenge, and choices. You can accept it or reject it; it's your choice. If you embrace the challenges of change, you can learn to succeed as you *grow* through the changes, not just *go* through the changes. And when your attitude is great, you can learn to accept and embrace the fact that change is a good thing. When you realize that change is an ally—not the enemy—and develop skills for managing change, your life will change and how you see life will change.

Famed poet Maya Angelou said it so wonderfully when she said, "If there is something in your life you don't like, change it. If you cannot change it, change your attitude!" I recommend that you decide to see change from a positive perspective. Stop right here and repeat after me: Change is good—when your attitude is great! Say it again: Change is good—when your attitude is great!

• • •

We've looked in this chapter at how people individually can respond to change, but this also applies to organizations, because organizations are made up of individuals. The attitudes and actions of an organization's people bring about—or inhibit—an organization's success. Five-star organizations are made up of people who know that change is going to happen whether they like it or not. They know that change is inevitable but that their response to it is up to them. They decide to embrace change and the challenges it brings. They see change as a friend, not a foe; as an ally, not an enemy. They know that all progress is the result of change. Great organizations are made up of people who don't let the "change train" pass them by. They jump on and drive the change train.

A critical part of the five-star success formula is understanding the importance of change. Winners understand that you must constantly get better in order to maximize your success, and in order to get better you must be willing to change.

Creating a "Teamwork Makes the Dream Work" Culture

Think Like a Team, Work Like a Team, Win Like a Team

I recently saw a great sign from a company that read: "We Are One Organization! We Are One Team! Yet We Have Unlimited Opportunities for Everyone on the Team to Win Personally . . . When We Work Together!" This quote emphasizes the incredible power of teamwork. Is it any wonder that this company exceeds the level of excellence of its competitors on a consistent basis?

Lance London, a dynamic serial entrepreneur who built a successful restaurant chain and then a successful pet food company, is quick to say that his success is always built on the power of his team. He is known to say, "It takes teamwork to make the dream work!" He's right. It truly does take teamwork to make the dream work. Those who think like a team and work like a team are those who *win* like a team!

Working with Diverse Teams

One of the persistent challenges of developing great organizations is to blend different people with different backgrounds and different personalities into a cohesive, homogenized unit. A critical component of the success journey that is often marginalized is the issue of learning to win with people who are different from you. Some people call this concept diversity, others call it inclusion, but those who understand the science of success call it good business!

I have learned that diversity in America is usually thought of in terms of ethnicity or gender, but my research has shown me that diversity is an issue that is seen in other countries and cultures as well. In some countries diversity is focused on height, or family background, or language variations within a country. The bottom line in the success process, however, is that this is not about ethnicity, gender, or any other difference; it is really about business and improving performance, productivity, and bottom-line profits.

In my interviews with successful businesspeople on the subject of diversity, one CEO said, "The number of people of color and different orientation is growing rapidly. I do not see diversity as being about kumbaya but rather it is about smart business practices—and I am in business to win, and look for people who might be different than me, but who also want to win!"

The words *diversity* and *inclusion* are often criticized and marginalized, because for so long they have been associated with "forced acceptance" rather than seen as a good business practice that can positively impact productivity and profits. A few years ago, I was asked to be the closing speaker for the Society for Human Resource Management's Annual Diversity Conference. I don't consider my message to be a diversity message, but it does help people to think differently about success and how everyone is important, no matter their color, background, or gender. So, in preparing for the conference, I made a point of interviewing a number of diversity experts from different industries. With each interview, I became more intrigued with the information I was presented with.

One expert told me that diversity work is really "mission work" because so many people who are asked to attend diversity trainings make up their minds they are not going to buy into the diversity concepts even before they go to the meetings. They make up their minds that they are going to put their sticks in the ground and refuse to change. They are hesitant to change and operate differently than their regular routine.

Those who lead the diversity operation must be patient and wise; they must help people see that this way of thinking can have a positive impact on their lives and their incomes. Joe Watson, the author of the best-selling book *Without Excuses: Unleashing the Power of Diversity to Build Your Business*, wrote,

"Diversity, like gravity, is all around us, and is therefore beyond dispute or debate. The challenge of leveraging that diversity and inclusion remains unfinished and unfulfilled! It is hard work!"

Watson went on to say, "Creating a diverse workforce is not about 'being nice,' but is rather about creating great business results. Between the pressure of global competition and emerging markets we must appreciate and look at all of the possibilities for continuing to expand and grow our businesses. Diversity and inclusion are not about being nice but rather about using all the possibilities for innovation, and that simply make sense . . . dollars and sense!"

In my speeches, I share a little anecdote that takes me back to my days as a jazz singer. I split the audience down the middle and tell them I am going to teach them how to sing jazz. I ask the right side of the audience to repeat after me as I sing a simple scat line that says, "Do wop!" Then I ask the left side of the audience to sing a difference scat line that says, "Do da!"

After teaching them their "parts," I tell them why it is important that I teach them this jazz song in this message about developing an attitude of excellence and building great teams. As I point to the audience, I get them to sing "their" part in a call-and-response manner. Finally, I add an a cappella bass line and get everyone singing in a round-robin manner and get them to snap their fingers, and, presto, we have a beautiful song! I then share with them that jazz is a music idiom that was created in America by African Americans. I explain why I believe it is important that we all learn more about African American culture, but we must not stop there! We, as Americans, need to know more about Asian Americans, and Hispanic/Latino Americans, and Jewish Americans, and East Indian Americans, and Arab Americans, and European Americans, and all the other people who are part of America. Why? Because although we might have come over here on different boats, we are in the same boat now. So we need to learn to row together!

Finally, I ask, "Do you see a band standing at the podium with me?" They all say no. And I say, "But we just made music!" In that group we were people of different ages, different colors, different genders, different religions, different orientations, different educations; yet when we worked together we made music. It is like a symphony orchestra, in which different types of instruments alone can make individual sounds, but together they can make harmony. Working together in a harmonious manner creates success and symphonic wonder. On the other hand, being distracted by differences and working against each other creates dissonance and noise. I recommend we learn to work, sing, play, and prosper together.

Prosper Together

Great organizations understand the power of the team and understand that to maximize their impact they must work together like a well-oiled machine. Great organizations know that everyone is an MVP, because the chain is only as strong as the weakest link. No one is an island and no one stands alone!

Team First, Individual Second

We have all heard the axiom that the acronym TEAM stands for Together Everyone Achieves More; and there is no "I" in TEAM. Yet I believe it is more complicated than that. Everyone has individual goals and dreams that can connect with the goals and dreams of the organization. The key is for leaders to develop the philosophy that as the team grows and prospers, so can everyone else grow and prosper. If you are going to have a five-star organization, it is critical that you make the commitment to develop a team that thinks about the team first and individual accomplishments second.

It is also critical to inspire the team to see how they can personally benefit from the success of the team as a whole. Over the last few football seasons, we have seen Super Bowl teams that win with few superstars on the teams—but there were many committed players. Those players were not household names, but they won because they made the commitment to think, "Team first." Because of that commitment, they often beat the teams with the big name players. As a result, those "no-name" players got more endorsement deals and more individual recognition, because they focused on winning as a team and then they won individually as well.

Everyone's Valuable

When I interviewed General Colin Powell on my Sirius XM show, he made a poignant point about the power of working together as a team. He said, "Success comes from a mindset of one team, one fight! Organizations that resemble warring tribes usually fail. Teams that fight as one cohesive unit tend to win!" I recommend you decide to work like a team and you will win more in both professional and personal terms.

This lesson is very evident in the story of the Chicago Bulls during the time of Michael Jordan and Phil Jackson. There was a young man from North Carolina named Michael Jordan, a first-round draft pick for the Chicago Bulls. When he joined the Bulls, he became a scoring machine and an instant success. He could score anytime he chose to, and he consistently led the league in scoring. But the team was never able to win a championship because it was a one-man team! No matter how many points he scored, the other team would score more because it was basically one man against a team of five. Even though Michael Jordan was an all-star defensive player, he could not guard five people. The opponents would come down the court, pass the ball around, and play team ball to outscore the Bulls because the Bulls were not a cohesive unit that worked together.

After a number of seasons of losing, the Bulls brought in a new head coach who had a new way of thinking, a team-minded approach to the game. This coach's name was Phil Jackson. His very first job was to convince Michael Jordan and then the rest of the team that the team that thinks like a team and works like a team is the team that will win. Phil Jackson took personal time with Michael Jordan and shared with him the merits of thinking and working like a team, including that, if the team won, Michael would personally benefit. At that point Michael Jordan was one of the highest-paid players in the league, yet Phil Jackson was able to convince him of the merits of thinking and working like a team! Jackson convinced Jordan that if they could think like a team and work like a team, they would also win like a team!

Phil Jackson brought in a number of new people, each with different areas of expertise, who could help to develop this new team. Some were ball handlers, some were defensive experts, and some were three-point shooters. All of them understood that if they kept the team focus and did their individual jobs effectively, the team could win. The Chicago Bulls went on to win three championships. Then Michael Jordan retired to play baseball. After a short time, he apparently preferred the basketball court to a baseball diamond and he donned the Chicago Bulls uniform once again and led the team to three more championships.

By the time Michael finally retired from the Bulls, his personal income was approximately ten times what it was before the team started winning! As the team won, so did Michael! If you can think like a team and work like a team, you can also win like a team. And you will personally benefit from the success of the team.

There is one more great lesson from those Chicago Bulls. Great teamwork involves having people on the team who make the decision that they want to win badly enough to get past their individual issues and agendas. This takes a conscious decision to talk *to* each other instead of talking *at* and *about* each other!

The Bulls had an infamous player named Dennis Rodman. He had a reputation for not being a team player. He consistently did his own thing, which was sometimes detrimental to the teams he played on. Yet, when he came to the Bulls, things changed. He became a committed team player! He would occasionally do unconventional things during his time off, but when he put on the Bulls uniform, he became a committed part of the Bulls team. What was the difference between Rodman's detrimental team concept with earlier teams in his career and his time with the Chicago Bulls? The difference was the Bulls' philosophy on the importance of the team. In Rodman's prior teams, he was criticized and talked "at" rather than encouraged and talked "to." Playing for the Bulls, he was constantly reminded that there was a benefit to each person on the team if the team won. If he started to drift back into his former patterns, he was reminded that he was a valued and important part of the team. He was appreciated and they depended on him to win!

And it was not just that he was reminded; it was also important how he was reminded, of his importance to the team and the importance of him being a team player. There was no talking behind his back, or sending out demeaning memos about him. Rather, the Bulls valued taking the time to sit down with

Rodman, person to person, to let him know that he was valued and important to the success of the team. Once Dennis Rodman was encouraged, then the criticisms that followed were easier for him to take and he was less defensive and resistant.

I must note that you might not make more money or have greater promotions or prestige, but I can attest that as the team grows, you, too, will grow. You'll be able to use the techniques and strategies you acquire in the organization to influence your family life and community activities. As the team prospers and grows, so will you!

Learning to Care for Your Teammates

The next part of the team-building journey is that great teams understand the chain is only as strong as the weakest link; therefore, each "link" must bond with the other links in a solid and secure manner. This connection requires developing a relationship that is trusting and secure among the different links. Believe it or not, many people do not participate in teams because they do not feel they are an equal part of the team and do not feel appreciated. To counter that, each individual within the organization should be appreciated for what they bring to the team and each individual also needs to make the commitment to develop a strong connection with the others so they can collaborate for greater success.

Developing Honest Communication

Far too often people hear about their shortcomings through memos or through secret watercooler conversations rather than through open and direct communication from a caring and concerned team member. Talking behind people's backs will lead to an unraveling of the moral fabric of the organization. It is critical to be open and honest and to be upfront about your concerns instead of talking behind the back of a coworker.

Steven Gaffney, the author of the book *Honesty Works*, surveyed people in the organizations that he works with and he found that more than 70 percent of the people who had major issues said they often withheld information or didn't tell the truth.

Many of these organizations bring him in to help them turn their companies around because of sagging profits. After he has worked with companies on the need for honest communications between coworkers, there is a dramatic improvement in their performance and profitability. Steven says that often the root cause of productivity problems is the lack of open and honest communication. Not just the truth versus lies aspect, but also withholding information and behind-the-back conversations. Plus, this lack of communication leads to fuzzy and blurred goals and expectations. In order to successfully collaborate, it is necessary to cooperate.

Steven writes, "Often it is not what team members say that is the problem, but rather what they don't say!" The key is to get the "unsaid" said, to get it spoken and not hidden. For example, when people are not performing well, people beat around the bush, dance around the issue, and talk behind people's backs instead of talking directly to each other. If people are not aware of what the problem is, then they cannot fix it. This is toxic to teamwork and the growth of the business. There are three things that have to happen to develop a culture of honest communication:

1. You must be aware of the problem. You cannot fix what you don't know.
2. Leaders must model the behavior of honest communication. Far too often, leaders say all the right things, but they do not *do* all the right things!
3. Employees must develop the ability to bring up the difficult issues. They also must be willing to be honest and direct in a caring and considerate way.

Open and honest communication can literally transform an organization and help teams to grow, even in the most difficult of times.

In regard to how you handle the difficult conversations, I recommend a technique that I explain it my marriage book, *Make Love, Make Money, Make It Last*. My wife and I share in the book that there are three big boulders that break up marriages—sex, money, and communication. Actually, the one that is most important of the three is communication, because if you have good communication, you can usually work out the problems with the first two issues. In order to have great communication in any relationship, whether it is personal or business, there are four points we recommend that you employ. They are:

1. Be Friendly: Never start any conversation in a hostile manner because it creates a defensiveness that alters the context of the conversation. The focus goes to the hostility rather than focusing on the real issues that need to be communicated and resolved.

2. Be Frank: Be honest, tell the truth, and tell how the situation made you feel and how the situation is impacting the relationship or impacting progress.

3. Be Fair: Be willing to listen and hear the other person's side, and take into account their perspective. Try seeing the situation from their perspective so you can see why they are thinking and feeling as they do.

4. Be Focused on a Positive Result: Winners always try to figure out how they can create win/win situations. The greatest negotiators always look for how they create a negotiation where everyone leaves the table feeling that they won.

Showing Appreciation for Team Members

In addition to communication, simple appreciation is a key element of a winning team. Simple appreciation is a powerful tool for building a winning organization. I believe that most people go to bed each night hungry—not for food, but for appreciation—that is to say, the simple expression of showing that you value the actions of another. That appreciation can have a tremendous impact on your long-term success and profits.

Some years ago, I was running late for a flight out of the Washington, DC, Dulles International Airport. I left the office in a hurry (as I often do) trying to get to the airport in evening rush hour traffic. While en route, unbeknownst to me, Shirley, my assistant, had called the airport to see if they could hold the plane for me. (She didn't know I had a deal with the airlines; if I am not there when they are ready to leave, they can leave without me.) After calling the airport, she called me in the car and said, "Willie, I called the airport to check on your flight and they told me it was an hour delayed. Take your time."

Before she hung up I said, "Wow! That's awesome. I won't have to drive like a crazy man, and I can even stop and get a soft drink. By the way, I just want to let you know that I really appreciate you." I hung up and stopped for the soft drink and got to the airport with plenty of time to spare.

When I finally returned to my office, there was a bouquet of roses on my desk. I assumed it was from a client, but when I read the note, I found my assistant had signed it! Completely perplexed, I asked why she'd given me the roses. She quickly replied, "Willie, before I came here to work, I worked at the same place for over ten years. Not once in those ten years did anyone say thank you!" Wow!

What a tremendous lesson I learned that day. I learned that a word of appreciation can change lives and encourage and inspire your team members to keep going even in challenging times. If you show appreciation on an "ongoing basis," you will find that the team will grow stronger and stronger.

Covering for Each Other

We are all aware that we have problems and personal issues that go with living. That is why I believe that everyone on every team has two jobs—that's right, two jobs! They have one job with the organization and then another job when they get home. They might go home to deal with elderly parents, mates who have physical or emotional problems, or teenagers (who might think they know more than you do).

I don't know what challenges await you at home, but I do know that everyone has some issues that impact their lives, not just at work but also at home. There will be times when you have a specific issue that is so painful you cannot even discuss it. And that is the day when you need your teammates to support you!

A friend of mine, who is a very successful corporate executive, called recently. His only sister had just died, and he needed a moment to talk with me. He knew I would understand, for I had lost my mother, my only brother, and my father-in-law within twenty-five days of each other. I shared with him how I was able to get through that challenging time and gave him some strategies for healing his broken heart.

He expressed that this was the most challenging time of his life, and that he was having a tough time at work. Initially, he did not tell his boss about his loss, and his boss came to him and asked if all was okay at home, because he was not working with the same efficiency as usual. He told his boss about the loss of his sister. His boss offered him time off if he wanted or needed it. It was left up to my friend to continue to work or to take some time off.

He chose to continue working. He realized that if he stayed home, he would just think about his sister and grieve all day. He wanted to stay at work, and even though his performance was not up to par, he would do the best he could. The boss and the team rallied around and covered for him. He shared with me how very much he appreciated his boss and teammates. He felt that they went above and beyond the call of duty.

We find that most work teams do *not* rally around their hurting teammates; instead, most work teams instead criticize their performance. My friend's group, however, was among the elite. They did what great teams do: cover for each other. Everyone is going to have one of those days when they have a challenge that is so painful and distracting that they need the support of the team to help them when they are not at their best.

Encouraging One Another

Years ago, I read an article about team building that shared lessons we can learn from geese. Geese fly in a "V" pattern because they have a goal, and as a team they know where they are going. They also fly in a "V" because they know if they work together and fly together, they can go farther and go faster with less effort than if they were flying alone. The harder they work together, the higher they fly together.

Then the article addressed the point that geese sometimes fly with and sometimes against the winds. When flying against the wind, the goose at the front of the "V" position has the most difficult position because it has to hit the headwinds. Yet the interesting phenomenon is that they rotate. Every goose gets a turn at the front position, a chance to hit the headwinds. Not only does it allow every goose an opportunity to rest from the challenges of the headwinds, but more importantly, it allows every goose a chance to get stronger.

Stronger how? In the process of hitting the headwinds, the goose strengthens its wings. Just as we would lift weights if we wanted to get stronger, they get stronger by facing the headwinds. "The stronger the breeze, the stronger the trees!" one old saying goes. It is through adversity that we grow and get stronger.

Another phenomenon about the geese flying in a "V" is that they tend to make a lot of noise as they fly. If you've ever noticed geese flying overhead, then you've probably noticed that they make so much noise that you can hear them honking from quite a distance. Recently I was in Williamsburg, Virginia, and I heard a lot of honking and squawking and looked up to see a flock of geese flying toward me in their formation. As they passed overhead, I realized that they weren't just passing time by honking and squawking—they were talking to each other:

"Go ahead, Greta, I've got your back!"

"Keep hitting those headwinds, George. We know you can do it!"

They were not just squawking; they were encouraging each other!

Vince Lombardi was right when he said great teams always care for each other, cover for each other, and encourage each other!

Win Together

If you want to learn to win, then you need to model those who have learned to win and have created a winning atmosphere—an atmosphere where everyone wins. One such role model is Bill Russell, the Hall of Fame basketball player who was the center for the professional basketball team with the greatest number of wins of all time. He is an example of someone who learned the secrets to winning and made every team he played on become a better team. He taught his teams how to think and win like a team. He helped create an atmosphere where winning became the norm and everyone on the team benefited. Bill Russell was not a superstar who started with a high demand to be on a winning team, but he worked on a philosophy where winning became a part of the culture.

As a high school graduate, Bill Russell needed a scholarship to go to college. Because was tall he thought he could possibly make the college basketball team. He got on the team as a walk-on. But he went from being a walk-on to leading the team to two NCAA championships. From there he was drafted into the NBA by the Boston Celtics and he led them to eleven championships in thirteen years!

What was most amazing about Bill Russell was that he was not a prolific scorer, but rather a player who focused his energy on creating a winning culture. Russell said he was not about scoring, but about winning. In his book, *Russell Rules,* he wrote, "Everyone can win, but it takes teamwork. Then you must add three key ingredients . . . attitude, aptitude, and appetite!"

A teachable person, with a positive attitude, can develop aptitude, especially if they have a strong appetite, a strong "I'll do anything it takes to win" drive. If you can accept the "good, better, best, never let it rest, until your good is better and your better is best" principle, then you can develop skillsets that will help you create a reputation for excellence.

If you are going to have five-star success professionally, it is important that you embrace the personal benefits and power of working as a team. I recommend you remember how important it is to care for your teammates, cover for them, and make a point to encourage them! It will help you win quicker and more often! Also remember how it is important to talk *with* each other, not talk *at* each other. Express your personal appreciation to your teammates, let them know that you value them, and treat everyone as integral to the success. Lastly, take a page from Bill Russell's playbook: Make a commitment to building a winning team. If your team prospers, you prosper; as your team grows, you grow.

Amaze the Customer with "WOW!" Service

Not *Good* Customer Service but *WOW* Customer Service

ustomer service is more than a cute term. It is a critical part of business success. It is the distinction that separates the good from the great. And you need more than *good* customer service; you need even more than *really good* customer service. You need WOW customer service! If you wow your customers with amazing service, your business will grow. If you wow your customers, they will in turn become not only loyal customers but will in effect become unpaid marketers for you. If you wow them, they will tell others and do so with such enthusiasm that those other people will want to experience the wow for themselves.

Five-star organizations constantly focus on how they can better serve their customers. They ask the questions "How can we improve our service today?" and "How would we like to be served?" The CEO of a five-star resort told me, "We are working to create a business that is so superior in our customer service that we embarrass our competition!"

I'm not talking about good customer service. I'm talking about astounding customer service that makes the customer say, "Wow, that was amazing!" If they say it to themselves, they will probably say it to their friends, too. Superior service that astounds is the secret to five-star organizations!

Service Is an Honor!

Martin Luther King, Jr. taught a powerful lesson about service in his last sermon at Ebenezer Baptist Church in Atlanta, not long before he was assassinated in Memphis. His sermon was called "The Drum Major Instinct" and during that sermon he shared a lesson about how greatness is really about service. In that sermon he said:

> Jesus gave us a new definition of greatness. If you want to be important, that's wonderful. If you want to be recognized, that's wonderful. But recognize that he who is greatest among you shall be your servant. That's a new definition of greatness; it means that everybody can be great, because everybody can serve. You don't have to make your subject and your verb agree in order to serve. You don't have to know about Plato and Aristotle to serve. You don't have to know Einstein's theory of relativity to serve. You don't have to know the second law of thermodynamics in physics to serve. You only need a heart full of grace and a soul generated by love,

and you can be that servant. If you can serve someone,
then you can be great!

While on a speaking tour in Japan, I had an experience that
changed my thinking about the incredible power of customer
service. Sometimes it is the small things that can make the biggest difference. Someone said that everything we need to be
successful we learned as children. I don't know if that is true,
but I do know that some important life lessons about success
can be quite simple.

After a two-week tour in Okinawa, Japan, to speak to the
U.S. Marines, my wife and I were scheduled to travel to Seoul,
South Korea. When we arrived at Nagasaki airport for our
flight, a representative of Korean Air met us. She bowed as we
entered, took our tickets, and said, "Hello! We have been waiting for you!"

I turned to my wife and said, "Wow, this is great! It must
be because I was the speaker, or because we have business class
tickets." The lady handed us off to another Korean Air representative who helped us check our luggage. After our bags
were checked, yet another Korean Air representative appeared
to escort us to what she said was the "VIP Waiting Area."

We now felt extra special as we walked toward the VIP
room. In order to get to the "VIP Waiting Area" we had to
walk past the entrance and the Korean Air representative we
had met when we first arrived. As we walked by, we overheard

the lady who had just greeted us say to another group, "We've been waiting for you!" We then realized that she said that to everyone. When we got to the VIP room, we found that it was a waiting room for everyone.

The Korean Air staff served cookies, small sandwiches, and soft drinks while we waited in the reception area with the rest of the passengers. We were all impressed with the service. It really was first-class service, but little did I know that the best was yet to come.

After a short time, we were told by other Korean Air representatives that they were there to escort us to the shuttle. They took us through security, then quickly through customs and directed us to the shuttle bus. Once we were all on the bus and it was ready to leave for the plane, the entire staff lined up alongside the bus. Every person we had met that day was there, from the Korean Air representative at the entrance to the person who checked our luggage to the people who took us to the waiting room to the ladies who escorted us from the VIP area. They all lined up next to the bus and as the shuttle bus was about to pull off, they bowed and said, "Thank you for letting us serve you!" Wow! The next time I travel to Korea, which airline do you think I will request? I'm requesting the one that gave me a "WOW" experience!

The awesome lesson I learned that day: It is an honor to be able to serve! I believe that whatever we do for a living, we should do it with a spirit of service. We should see our jobs as not just work, but as an honor and a time to serve. Since that experience in Japan, every time I give a speech I do not see it as work but rather as an opportunity to serve.

I heard my friend, the late, great Cavett Robert, founder of the National Speakers Association, say, "Service is the rent we pay for our place on this earth!" I could not agree more.

Winning Over Your Customers

If we want to win more, we must think differently about the word *win*. We traditionally think of the word *win* with regard to personal success or gaining an advantage over another person or organization. But I believe there is another perspective we should consider. Five-star organizations have expanded their thinking of the word *win* to include a commitment to do whatever is necessary to serve the customer. For great organizations to win, they need to win over customers. If they are to win over customers, they need to do whatever is necessary to serve them. Think of it as an acronym: WIN, Whatever Is Necessary. They understand that amazing customer-centric service is the key to gaining the ultimate advantage over their competitors. To do "whatever is necessary" to serve the customer is a major part of creating your own culture of excellence and five-star success story.

My friend T. Scott Gross, the author of the hugely popular P.O.S. (Positively Outrageous Service) book series, says that in today's marketplace we cannot settle for being good or very good; we must strive for Positively Outrageous Service, which is service that goes beyond expectations. It is service that astounds and amazes the customers. So make up your mind to do Whatever Is Necessary to astound your customer through Positively Outrageous Service!

Keep Wooing Your Customers: Don't Let the Romance Die!

I wrote an article for a Valentine's Day column and the response was so overwhelming that I thought you would enjoy reading how success in business and in life are about not letting the romance die. I even wrote about it in our first marriage book, *Make Love, Make Money, Make It Last!* It has since been a popular part of our marriage series, available at www.jolleymarriage. com (feel free to visit and get a free chapter from the book):

> Friend, it is important to keep in mind that we should not just be thinking of romance around Valentine's Day! We should be thinking about romance all year long! To have a healthy and vibrant relationship, the romance should be ongoing. And in order to keep the fires burning, you must be willing to make an "ongoing commitment" to never-ending romance!

I have been married for more than thirty years to the one and only Ms. Dee, and learned early on to commit to never letting the romance die. When I first got married, I had a conversation with an older man, who had been married for more than fifty years. He and his wife acted like newlyweds. So I asked him what was the secret to the excitement that he and his wife shared. He said, "Love is not just an emotion; it is a decision."

He went into great detail on how to keep those love fires burning. Suffice it to say, he taught me that a "happy wife creates a happy life!" He helped me realize that it takes a commitment to romance your mate daily—not just on Valentine's Day or birthdays, but every day!

Take time out every day to tell your mate that you love them. Make time for a "date night" once a week. Dee and I have been married for more than thirty years and have not had an argument in over twenty-five years. The first few years were like World War III, but we learned some principles that work, and one of them is to have a date night weekly. When our kids were little, and we could not afford any date nights out, we would have date time in front of the television, with our bedroom door open! We'd eat popcorn, watch television, and talk! It was our time alone, and it has continued throughout the years.

I share all this because the same is true for our business. Just as we never let the romance die for our marriage, we must do the same with our clients. We must work hard to keep that business romance from dying. Unfortunately, many people work hard to get the business, but stop courting their clients once they get their business. My office manager recently changed office suppliers. After she made the change, the old supplier sent an email asking, "What did we do to lose your business? We didn't do anything bad!" My office manager simply replied, "Right! You didn't do anything bad . . . In fact, you simply didn't do anything—and that was the problem! You worked to get our business and then we rarely heard from you."

Statistics show that it costs twice as much to get new clients as it does to keep old ones. And we all know that in love relationships, it's "cheaper to keep them!" So work at keeping the romance alive, at home and in business. Keep courting them and letting them know you appreciate them. The rewards are endless!

"Yes" Is the Answer . . . Now What Is the Question?

I was speaking for the Human Resource Organization of Central Ohio for my friend Stan Robbins, and he and I had dinner at the Fish Market Restaurant in Columbus, Ohio. During dinner, Mike Frank, who is a former president of the National Speakers Association, joined us and Mike and Stan shared stories about the restaurant and its incredible customer service. They mentioned how the owner, Cameron Mitchell, had started a chain of restaurants that was focused on great food and incredible customer service. His motto was "The answer is 'Yes' . . . Now what is the question?"

Mike shared a story of how he and his wife were at the restaurant one night and he had a taste for macaroni and cheese, but it was not on the menu. He asked the server if it was possible to have macaroni and cheese, even though it was not on the menu. Though it was not something they usually served, the server said, "The answer is yes! We can make that happen." And they did! She went in the back and told the cooks about the order for macaroni and cheese. They did not have the ingredients available, so they called another restaurant close by who specialized in macaroni and cheese and ordered some. Then they had a driver run and get it and bring it back piping hot. Mike said it was delicious and hit the spot, but more importantly, it taught him a valuable lesson about service. Organizations that want to wow the customer find a way to say, "Yes" to them.

The Ten Commandments of Superior Service

Over my many years as a professional speaker, I have worked with many major corporations considered to be "five star." While working with these organizations I have found that customer-centric service is an integral part of each of their cultures. It is not just something they talk about in quarterly meetings, but something that they talk about every day and that they exhibit in every interaction with customers. They develop their people and start them from day one with a mindset to astound the customers.

Yet, there are also high-impact organizations that have the customer service conversation, and the people want to serve the customers with excellence, but unfortunately they don't know how to serve the customers with excellence. We often see this in organizations that rely on volunteer service (like churches). We often find workers in volunteer organizations who have the will to serve, but lack the skill to serve. They have a heart to serve, but they have never been given the training and tools to serve at the highest levels. We often find nice people who want to grow their churches and volunteer organizations, but they are ill-equipped to follow through on the dictates that are coming from the leaders and from the pulpit.

Far too often we see great preachers who are working hard on the message that inspires the listeners, but are undermined by poor customer service from the church workers, who are willing but unable to effectively serve at the highest levels. Why? Because they are unsure how to deliver world-class service. They need the skill to go with the will.

So I want to show them, and you, how. Here are my ten commandments for superior service. (I speak at a lot of churches, so I have created a special scriptural verse for each commandment for those who feel a commandment needs to be supported by scripture. You can get that special scriptural verse version as a gift from me to you at www.attitudeofexcellence.com.)

Commandment #1—Thou Shalt Serve with a Smile

Scripture teaches that the greatest leaders are always the greatest servants. And those who make a commitment to serve do so with a spirit of joy. As a result they serve with a smile. Why smile? It is important to smile because a smile expresses a sentiment that words often cannot express, such as, "I am pleased you're here. I want to help you," or "It makes my day to be able to help make your day!" This is why most companies stress "service with a smile." In fact, there is an old Jewish proverb that states, "A person who cannot smile should not open a store!"

It is possible to smile even when you must share information that is not to the person's liking (e.g., "I am sorry, but you cannot park there. You must park in the overflow lot and catch the bus."). If you can learn to smile, even when you have to say no, then you will catch the spirit of five-star organizations. Practice saying no while smiling. It will help you as you move to become an effective leader.

Commandment #2—Thou Shalt Go the Extra Mile

In his book *Positively Outrageous Service*, T. Scott Gross writes, "One of the keys to success in serving others is to make a commitment to always go the extra mile with your customers." Five-star organizations understand that and they always, constantly and consistently, go the extra mile. Here is an example of one organization going the extra mile for me when I was their customer. I was scheduled to speak once for the United States Army in San Diego, California, the fourth of five cities I was scheduled to visit on that speaking tour. I arrived at my five-star hotel feeling terrible. I had chills and my throat felt scratchy. At the reception desk, the hotel clerk greeted me with a note concerning a client dinner that I was invited to attend later that evening. When she noticed I was feeling poorly, she asked if I was okay. I told her that I was tired and feeling a little under the weather so I was going to forego the dinner and go to bed. I hoped I would feel better in the morning, in time for my program.

Almost immediately after I arrived at the room, there was a knock on the door. When I opened it, there was a waiter with a big bowl of chicken soup. He said, "We hope this makes you feel better. Have a good night's sleep!" The soup was perfect for my travel-weary body. The next morning, I was feeling as good as new.

Those who are willing to go the extra mile are those who will win more consistently day in and day out. There is a story that my wife witnessed, and it inspires me. I have shared it with audiences all over America. My wife went to the post office near our home. The two women who run that post office make everyone who comes there feel like family. These ladies always ask how you and your family are doing. They call people by name.

One day at this post office, my wife noticed a Hispanic man at the counter and that one of the ladies was trying to explain to him that he did not have appropriate information to get his order completed. After realizing the gentleman did not speak English, and was not able to understand her, she did something remarkable. She came from around the counter and took him by the hand. She led him outside of the post office and took him next door, where there was a Spanish restaurant. Some of the folks at the restaurant spoke Spanish and one of them translated for her, so she could serve the customer with the spirit of excellence. She was able to communicate with the gentleman and share the information he needed. Then she took him by the hand and led him back into the post office and helped him get the mailing he needed. That is going the extra mile!

In order to create a five-star life, you must make a commitment to do more than what is necessary. Go the extra mile . . . There is never a traffic jam along the extra mile!

Commandment #3—Thou Shalt Greet, Speak, and Be Real Sweet!

Many leading banks have learned the power of greeting customers as they come in and some have actually been assigning greeters at the door. And, of course, the number-one retailer in the world, Walmart, which has built its business with lower prices and high customer service, has always had a greeter at the front to say "Hello!" to its customers. There is power in the first impression. The word *hello* is a powerful inducement for business growth. Just that one word!

Add to your greeting a commitment to be sweet to people—really sweet. People remember those who are nice, but they love those who are really sweet.

Several years ago at a men's conference at the Crystal Cathedral in Garden Grove, California, I visited the bookstore to get a specific book. I left with five! I didn't really need them, but the people there were so sweet that I just couldn't leave, and the longer I stayed, the more I spent! The cathedral had not only greeters, but also people who went out of their way to speak to you—people who were really sweet!

Commandment #4—Thou Shalt Say Thank You and Please—A LOT!

A popular inspirational book states, "The most important things you learn about success, you learn in kindergarten." It states that the basics of life are usually the keys to long-term success. In kindergarten, we were taught we must share and learn to get along with different people with different personalities. We learned that it is very important to say thank you and please, and to say these magic words a lot.

This isn't true just for success on the playground. In order to have a five-star organization, employees must get along with many different types of people and many different personalities. They need to say "thank you" and "please" a lot. These words of respect work as a tonic or oil that smoothes every working relationship.

If you want to have a five-star operation, it is crucial that you have five-star manners. Make good manners part of your standard operating procedure. Say "thank you" and "please" a lot.

Commandment #5—Thou Shalt Be Willing to Apologize Quickly!

Often, an apology is only given after a long, drawn-out confrontational experience, after which there is no other option but to apologize. This is not the best approach. If a customer is offended or there is a problem, don't make excuses and don't be confrontational; be willing to say, "I'm sorry," even if you are not at fault. Be willing to say, "I am sorry that happened" and "How can we make this right for you?"

A quick apology defuses potentially explosive and ugly situations. The organization never wins—even if they are in the right. Five-star organizations use the power of apologizing and are willing to apologize quickly. They don't delay the apology to prove they are right.

Bill Cates is one of America's premier referral experts. In his book *Get More Referrals Now,* he says that clients who share problems and complaints with you should be seen as a jackpot to grow your business! They are giving you insight into how to better your business. He writes:

In handling complaints you should:

1. Say "I'm sorry" and say it quickly. It should be the first thing out of your mouth. Why? Because it costs nothing to say I'm sorry. It is not admitting fault, but simply expressing that you feel sorry that they were inconvenienced.
2. Don't take it personally and get defensive. If you do, you're likely to make excuses and challenge their perceptions. This accomplishes nothing and makes the client feel as though you really are not there for them.
3. Don't argue. Nobody has ever won in an argument with a client. If you "win" and prove you are right and they are wrong, in reality you lose. Don't worry who is right or wrong; see how you can help them and find a solution to the problem.
4. Thank them for bringing the concern to your attention. Nothing is worse than having a major problem that others know about, but no one tells you about!
5. When you say you are sorry, say it like you mean it, not just trite words, but sincere sentiment.

A woman from California who had bought one of my books at a local bookstore called our office. When she got home and started going through the book, she realized there was a missing page. She looked on the internet for my information and called my office and brought the missing page to my attention. These books were printed, produced, shipped, and stocked in stores by my publisher, not by me. After I finished writing the manuscript, it was technically out of my hands. Yet, when she called, my team apologized for her inconvenience and sent her a new book! Why? Because even though it was not my fault that the book had a missing page and it was technically the publisher's responsibility, *my name was on that book.* I wanted to make things right with her.

People don't really care whose fault it is. They care about being treated kindly and being heard. Make a commitment to apologize, even if it is not your fault. Find a way to fix the problem as quickly as you can.

Commandment #6—Thou Shalt Anticipate

Anticipate the needs of your customers. Outstanding organizations don't just respond to the needs of their customers, they study their customers to plan ahead of their next move or need, so they are prepared to respond. Often I meet with clients over a meal to discuss their programs. Often they will suggest that we meet at five-star restaurants. One such restaurant is 1789 in Georgetown, Washington, DC. The food is always great there, but it's the service of this restaurant that's truly mind-blowing. They don't just respond to our needs; they hover at the table, waiting and planning ahead. Case in point: Rather than coming around and refilling our water glasses when they are empty, 1789 never lets the glasses get anywhere near empty. A napkin left on your chair (while you leave for the restroom) is replaced with a fresh one. The bread crumbs are swept from the table and used silverware disappears without a sound.

Five-star organizations look for ways to engage customers and meet their needs before they have to ask. You can follow their example. If you look for more ways and opportunities to anticipate the needs of your customers, you will see your reputation and your business grow.

Commandment #7—Do What Is Necessary, Not What Is Comfortable!

To succeed in life and in business, it is critical to go beyond our comfort zones! We must be willing to change and willing to stretch if we are going to grow. Whenever you change and stretch, you will be faced with challenges, both internal and external. An external challenge is the challenge we will face whenever we try something new and try to do different things. No matter what that change is, some people just don't like it because it is beyond their comfort zone.

Yet the biggest challenge we face in trying to change is internal. An old African proverb states, "If you can overcome the enemy on the inside, the enemy on the outside can do you no harm!" That internal challenge is getting yourself to believe that it is possible to change, stretch, and grow. Change is required to grow an organization to the next level, and that change will always create some opposition.

You must make the commitment to do what is necessary, not comfortable. I learned this lesson early in my speaking career when I was primarily speaking to youth groups. I was going from school to school speaking to young people. One day I went to an inner-city school. After going through the metal detectors, I was directed to the principal's office, where I had to ring a bell to be admitted! The principal looked through the blinds, cracked the door a little bit, and said, "Hurry in!" He asked, "How long will you be speaking?" I said "About an hour." He said, "If I were you, I would speak for fifteen minutes. These kids can't handle an hour-long speech. The last person who was here to speak lasted only about fifteen minutes before they got rowdy!"

As I heard my introduction being read, I wondered how I could cut my speech down to fifteen minutes, as the principal had suggested. I figured I could cut out the material on drug prevention, the section on alcohol, and the call for academic excellence and integrity, and just give them some flowery motivational quotes and go! But, as I got ready to speak, my spirit spoke to my heart and said, "What are you going to do today, Willie? Are you going to do what's comfortable or what's necessary?" Some of these kids have never heard a motivational speaker; some have never heard anyone who came out of this same inner-city environment, yet made a commitment to struggle through the academic process and succeed, or struggle with his communication skills to learn how to use words to positively influence people. "So Willie, what are you going to do today? Are you going to do what is comfortable or what is necessary?"

I spoke to those young people for an hour and a half, and when I finished, they gave me a standing ovation! I later learned a valuable lesson that in order to grow and make a difference, you must do what is necessary, not what is comfortable. We may need to have a conversation with ourselves as to what is the right action to take. We know the right actions, but must talk ourselves into acting. For we have fears of being embarrassed, rejected, failing, or being made fun of. Nevertheless, five-star organizations make a commitment to go with what is necessary, not what is comfortable. So must we!

Commandment #8—Thou Shalt Take Responsibility

To become an effective leader, you must respond with all your ability so you are empowered to take the necessary action to help customers without having to ask for permission to do the right thing. To take responsibility is to step out in faith as a leader and to be proactive in dealing with the needs of your customers. And remember, everyone has customers; they're the people who give your organization a reason to continue to function. No matter whether you work with a corporation, a church, a government agency, or a nonprofit, you exist to impact someone, and that someone is your customer.

To take responsibility means to go beyond job titles and job descriptions and think about what needs to be done and then go about doing it! Upon recently visiting a church, I witnessed an usher translating the sermon to a woman who was a Spanish speaker, word for word! Her job description, usher, did not include translation services, but she made the decision to take responsibility and respond with her ability. In doing so, she reached the guest in a way that she could understand and appreciate. In order to create a five-star organization, it is important that everyone make the same commitment to take responsibility and to respond with their ability. They must make the commitment to not just do their job, but to do whatever is necessary to get the job done, even if it is not in their job description!

Commandment #9—Thou Shalt Lighten the Lines!

No one—and I do mean no one—likes lines! Think about it: If you are at the grocery store, don't you look for the shortest line? If you are at a bank, doesn't it frustrate you if there are long lines? If you are traveling and come upon a traffic jam with a sea of red brake lights, don't you moan?

Statistics show that the main reason people change banks is not because of the interest rates or financial concerns, but because of the lines! Five-star organizations are always trying to find ways to lighten the lines.

If the lines cannot physically be shortened, then businesses do the next best thing: They talk to the people in the lines! They apologize and thank the customers for their patience. The employees make eye-contact with the customers in line and say things like, "We'll be right with you!"

I have had the opportunity to speak to popular five-star organizations, like Gaylord Hotels, and I can tell you that they really know how to handle lines. When their lines form as one group is checking out while another group is checking in, Gaylord employees walk up and down the lines and smile and speak to the customers. In addition to thanking the customers for their patience, they recognize the customers and acknowledge that they are important. A few smiles and a simple acknowledgment can do a lot to lessen the anxiety of the lines. If you can shorten the lines, or at least the anxiety that comes from them, you will grow your five-star status.

Commandment #10—Thou Shalt Practice the CANEI Principle

In the late 1940s and 1950s, the Japanese were recovering from World War II and struggling to survive. They started creating items to be sold overseas and always stamped the items as "Made in Japan." During those times, whenever people in America saw the "Made in Japan" stamp, they knew the items were of inferior quality and could be purchased inexpensively. This practice went on through the 1950s and early 1960s. In the late 1960s, something changed.

Dr. Edward Deming, a management guru, went to Japan and taught the Japanese an innovative concept called the "CANEI Principle"; CANEI is an acronym that stands for Constant and Never Ending Improvement. It means making a commitment to never be satisfied and to keep bettering your best on a daily basis. Within a decade of embracing this principle, the Japanese had gone from worst to first! Japanese electronics and automobiles dominated the marketplace, and still do so today.

Five-star organizations embrace this principle. This commitment to constant and never-ending improvement requires each person to ask: How can I do better tomorrow than I did today? Those who achieve great things in life understand the power of self-development and make a commitment to constant and never-ending improvement.

If you were able to achieve perfection, where would you go from there? Constant and never-ending improvement allows us to continue to improve as we strive for excellence. Once we achieve excellence, we are automatically compelled to try to constantly improve and better our best!

Great organizations never become satisfied. To create a five-star organization, it is critical to make a commitment to the CANEI Principle: constant and never-ending improvement. Get started today!

• • •

Those are the Ten Commandments for Outstanding Customer Service. If you use them, you will find that they will have a profound impact on your reputation, your productivity, and your profits.

The Customer Is Number One

I was speaking at Walmart headquarters in Arkansas when I realized that they didn't just happen to become the number-one retailer in the world by chance. Their philosophy of constant and never-ending improvement led them to their number-one status. I spoke at an awards banquet one Friday evening and was invited to stay around to attend the Saturday morning managers' meeting. It was an amazing experience to see managers and employees come in voluntarily on a Saturday morning. But, what was more amazing was how the company philosophy was embedded into the consciousness of the employees!

First, they all participated in the company cheer, which was a chant that goes like this: "Give me a W!" And the crowd responded, "W!" "Give me an A!" And the crowd responded, "A!" "Give me an L!" "L!" "Give me a squiggly!" (That was the hyphen that originally was used between the words Wal and Mart.) And all the people would do a little twist. "Give me an M!" "M!" "Give me another A!" "A!" "Give me an "R!" "R!"

"Give me a T!" "T!" "What does that spell?" And the crowd shouted, "Walmart!" "Again, what does that spell?" "Walmart!" "Who's number one?" and the next response truly blew my mind, because in unison they all screamed, "The *customer* . . . is *always* number one at Walmart!"

That experience made me realize that Sam Walton, the founder of Walmart, established a philosophy of customer service years ago that took him from a small five-and-dime store in a little city in Arkansas to becoming the biggest retailer in the world. He made a commitment to serve the customer and make sure that they were always the number-one focus. He also instilled an attitude of excellence, encouraging his employees to constantly pursue excellence.

At that same Saturday morning meeting, I was in awe as the Walmart employees chanted, "Good is the enemy of Best . . . and Best is the enemy of Even Better!" I agree wholeheartedly. The race for excellence has no finish line; no end point. With an attitude of excellence, there is never a point where you are ever "good enough!" Therefore, you must always keep working to get even better than best. We must not merely give great customer service; we must give awesome customer service. Service that is so memorable that the customer says, "Wow!" and then tells everyone they talk to about it. Yet we can't even stop there. We must bear in mind that every customer is important—whether he or she pays first-class, business-class, or coach-class prices!

We must thank them for their business! Remember that the big-time customers of today often started as the little customers who kept growing as they continued to do business with you.

Always provide a WOW experience for each and every one of your customers. Make sure to say thank you and let them know you appreciate the opportunity to serve them. In today's complex and competitive marketplace, it will definitely set you apart from the crowd.

Make a commitment to give wow customer service. You will be glad you did!

Develop a Never-Ending Winner's Attitude

Instill a Positive Attitude in Your Team

When I interviewed General Colin Powell on my Sirius XM show, he made the following comment: "Perpetual optimism is a force multiplier. Just as a home-team crowd is the twelfth person in a football contest, so too is optimism the extra force to help you win more in business and in life. In a winning operation it is critical to be optimistic!"

Optimism is indeed a powerful force, and it's a force that is available to each and every person and every organization. A positive attitude impacts every facet of life, and can help you to reach and exceed your goals more readily. A positive attitude can help you to win more. Now, that begs the question, "If I have a positive attitude, will I get everything that I want?" The answer is no, but you will get more than when you have a negative attitude.

A positive attitude can impact an organization in a unique way as well, by creating a positive work atmosphere, which is a powerful tool in developing a winning culture. This is why five-star organizations focus on their people's attitude. They know the attitude culture determines the success of an organization. Attitude is the lifeblood that keeps an organization moving.

Attitude Is the Oil of Achievement

I often ask the people in my audiences how many of them have cars. Most of the hands in the room go up. I ask them how often they change the oil in their cars. The usual answer is every three months or three thousand miles. I then ask what would happen if they decided to go a year or two without an oil change. Of course, the answer is that the car would run sluggishly and eventually break down.

I believe that the same is true for organizations. Attitude is the oil of achievement. If you don't do preventive maintenance on the attitude of the organization, in time the organization will slow down, start to run sluggishly, and eventually break down. There are far too many examples of organizations that have had no ongoing training programs for employees, and in the process there has been no way to enhance employee attitudes in terms of customer relations. As a result, negative, toxic influences creep in, and before long, the organization falls apart. Negative influences wear away at the fabric of an organization, and without attention to the details involved in employee attitude, those negative influences will unravel the fabric of that organization like a loose thread in a fine sweater.

Aptitude comes second, as we analyze employee attitude enhancement. Why? Because every director of five-star organizations I've interviewed said that a teachable person with a great attitude and limited aptitude is better than a person with great aptitude and a know-it-all or negative attitude. One of the surefire killers of an organization is a person with a funky, negative attitude. That negative attitude is like the flu: It is contagious and will decimate the workplace in no time. Attitude enhancement is critical for success.

Lee Iacocca, the savior of Chrysler Motor Cars, once said, "The kind of people I look for to fill our top management spots are the eager beavers, the mavericks, those who try to do more than they are expected to do . . . They always reach." He looked for people who created a reputation for excellence and had a positive attitude. People who succeed in the long run are those who have created a reputation for excellence over the long haul.

When you have a positive attitude, you will see change differently. Change becomes part of the growth process. You start to see that what is a negative situation for some people will turn out to be a positive one for you.

Make It Contagious: Catch the Excellence Attitude!

Five-star organizations have a very clear vision of where they are going; they share and articulate that vision to their entire company, and then they use excitement and enthusiasm to sell their people on it. Five-star organizations commit their resources to making the vision a reality. And once they start the quest for excellence, they take the next step, which is making a commitment to their commitment on a daily basis.

If organizations want employees to create a culture of excellence, they need for those in the organization to catch the "excellence attitude," and it starts with everyone knowing the organization's vision. Those who really connect with the company's vision realize that with an attitude of excellence it is quite possible to achieve goals that others consider impossible; this attitude of excellence will be contagious and spread throughout the team. But, in order for the team to connect with the vision, someone must first sell the vision. And before you can sell the vision to others, you must first sell the vision to yourself.

Typically, when we speak of the word *attitude* we refer to a disposition. When we think of a person having "an attitude," we generally think of the person having a bad or negative disposition. I believe that a negative attitude is "contagious" and can be transmitted from one person to another. Just as a person with a negative attitude can infect an organization and make it an unpleasant place to work, a person with a positive attitude— an attitude of excellence—can lift the spirit and climate of the organization and help foster an environment where people are excited about work and a free flow of new ideas is encouraged. The challenge is that people who are negative are usually willing to readily share their thoughts with others, while people with positive attitudes often tend to keep their thoughts to themselves or only express those thoughts to their close friends.

Change Your Attitude and Sell Your Way to Success

A positive attitude is not something that you need to be born with; it is something that can be learned. In the same way, you need not be a born leader; in fact, most leaders are not born but their leadership abilities are developed over time. So remember that you can learn to lead and you can learn to have a positive attitude. You can also learn to win more! Winners typically don't know how they are going to win, but they believe that somehow they will figure out a way to win. A winner has a positive attitude, which includes a positive outlook, a positive "in-look," and a positive "up-look." When you have a great attitude you can learn to see that change is good. When all is said and done, it's about your attitude!

A speaker friend called me one day, and during the conversation, he said, "You know, I love speaking, but right now we are having difficulty with our sales. Selling really sucks." As soon as he said it I knew why his sales were suffering. I told him, "If you ever want to have success in sales, you must never let those words come out of your mouth again. In fact, you can never let those words enter your thoughts! In order to have sales success you have got to learn to love it!"

I told him I learned that valuable lesson years ago when I was getting started on the speaking circuit and was getting on and off planes every day. At first, the travel was fun, but after about a year the traveling lost its glamour. It was around that time that I had a conversation with another speaker friend, the late, great Keith Harrell, the author of *Attitude Is Everything*, who was in such demand that he typically traveled over two hundred days a year. Keith and I were talking one day and I said, "Man, I hate this traveling!" Keith quickly responded, "Willie, you can never let those words come out of your mouth again, because whatever you speak is what eventually becomes your reality!"

Keith asked me a very pointed question. He said, "Willie, what do you love to do?" I said, "I love to speak and inspire people." He then said, "Do you agree that in order to do what you love to do, you might have to travel occasionally?" I said, "Well, yes!" He responded: "Then don't you agree that travel really is the price you must pay in order to get to do what you love to do?" I said, "Well, yes, that's true." Keith then said, "Then you can never ever say again that you hate to travel because travel is really just a price you pay to get to do what you love to do."

I told my friend who was lamenting that "selling sucks" that when I was in college, I took a logic class and I learned about deductive logic, which states that if Socrates is a man, and all men are mortal, then Socrates must be mortal. Going along the same lines of thinking, if he loved to speak (which he told me he loved to do), and if selling is what he must do in order to speak more, then logic would say that therefore he loved selling. He was quiet for a few seconds; then he said, "You know what, Willie? You are right!" He then proceeded to proclaim, "I love selling! I love selling! I love selling!" His sales started to improve because his attitude toward selling improved, and so did his income. He has since gone on to build a huge business, because he simply changed his attitude!

I like the old story of the young salesman who asked for a meeting with the CEO to discuss a raise. The young salesman asked, "I need more money, so when will I get a raise?" The CEO who had been in sales all his life responded, "My friend, your raise will become effective the moment you change your thinking and you become more effective." As his attitude improved, so did his income. What's the lesson? Work on your attitude! Decide to win. It will change your life.

If you love what you do for a living, and you must sell in order to do more of what you love to do, then logic would state that you therefore love selling. Go forth and sell with a passion because from here on, You Love Selling. Attitude is truly a major part of five-star success.

Let the Challenges Propel You to Your Next Level of Success

Life is filled with challenging times, yet you must not allow those challenges to stop you. Instead you should let them propel you to your next level of success. In chapter 2 of my book, *A Setback Is a Setup for a Comeback*, I say, "Some days you're the windshield, and some days you're the bug!" Some days, everything goes your way; and some days, you are faced with "1-800-Brickwall." But don't despair. Every day you wake up you get to choose. You get to choose to be a negative bug or you can choose to be a positive bug. It is your choice!

First, you must understand how a negative bug thinks. A negative bug wakes up, starts his or her day, and hits a windshield. The negative bug doesn't like the windshield, nor does it deserve the windshield, yet it happens, and the negative bug has to deal with the situation. The negative bug deals with the situation by crying and whining and complaining about the bad things that have happened, telling everyone who will listen how horrible his or her life is. The negative bug makes a habit of complaining. The negative bug doesn't know the real deal about what happens when you complain: 80 percent of the people you complain to simply don't care, and the other 20 percent are just glad it is not them. Eventually, the negative bug creates a downward spiral, and smashes, crashes, and burns.

The positive bug wakes up, starts out on his or her way, and also hits a windshield. The positive bug doesn't like and doesn't deserve the windshield, and yet it also has to deal with the windshield. But the positive bug has a different attitude. He or she realizes that the major key to long-term success is that while they cannot control what happens *to them*, and cannot control what happens *around* them, they have complete control over what happens *inside* of them. And they choose to be happy!

You have the same option! You can choose to be a positive person or a negative person. You can choose to look at life from a positive perspective or you can choose to see all the bad and stay focused on the negative parts of your life. You can whine and cry and complain about life and live a pitiful existence or you can choose to be grateful and refuse to let anything or anyone take away your joy. That is your choice. As a result of that choice, you can develop a force called resiliency, the ability to bounce back from adversity and difficult situations.

One more thing. While the negative bug smashes, crashes, spirals down, and burns, the positive, resilient bug bounces off the windshield. As a result of the slant of the windshield and aerodynamics, the positive bug bounces up and flies in a higher trajectory—and therefore flies above the other auto windshields. Occasionally, a tractor trailer will come along, but that is just another opportunity for the positive bug to fly even higher. Make the decision to stay positive and you will see how you will bounce off of situations and fly higher!

Stuff will happen and change will happen, but ultimately it is your choice as to how you respond to it. So don't take stuff personally, and whatever you do, don't let it stop you. Don't just go through it. Learn to *grow* through it!

In the book *The Road Less Traveled*, by Dr. M. Scott Peck, the first four words say it all. They are "Life is difficult . . . period!" Yes, life is difficult and can be challenging, yet life is still wonderful and awesome at the same time. I'm working on a new book that says it like this: "Life does not have to be perfect to be wonderful!"

Success is a choice and if you really want to succeed and live a life of five-star success, it all comes down to making good choices and not letting your life be governed by default, which means the status quo for all the negative thinkers who set the standard for complaining and whining about life. In other words, it will come down to your choices—you can listen to the negative voices on television and radio, or you choose to listen to the positive voices, like this book and other positive books. Remember, your attitude is your choice. You must make the choice to stay positive in spite of the challenges of life.

The third part of attitude enhancement, after aptitude, is you must have appetite. Appetite is your desire for your goals. What level of desire do you possess? What are you willing to do? How badly do you want to win? What are you willing to do to achieve your goal? This is an important question in the quest for five-star success. Imagine if someone took you out to Giants Stadium in the Meadowlands of New Jersey. And while you were standing in the middle of the field, the person said to you, "There is a treasure worth millions of dollars buried somewhere in this field, and I am offering you an exclusive opportunity to find it and claim it!" Would you be willing to start digging? I assume most people would say, "Yes, I would be willing!" The challenge is that you don't know where on that big field the money is buried. You very well could be digging for quite a while! The key to finding the money is the willingness to keep digging.

I contend that the same is true in life; you must keep digging for your millions. I believe that there are millions of dollars with your name on them, waiting for you to come up with an idea, product, or service that the world will pay you for, yet you must continue to keep digging. I don't know where the treasure is buried, but I do know where the key to the treasure is—the key is within you! And you must be willing to keep digging for it. My friend Bishop T.D. Jakes, noted preacher, author, and movie producer, tells me:

> Many wonder and talk about the fact that I just appeared one day and had success, but they did not see the years and years of struggle in the back hills of West Virginia. Everything I have achieved is a result of struggle and working hard to reach my goals. I have continued to dig and dig and dig! So when I die, make sure to look up under my fingernails. You will find dirt under my fingernails because I will be digging until the absolute end!

I encourage you to keep digging and to keep pursuing excellence as you go after your dreams and goals. You must want it badly and you must have a strong appetite. To live the five-star life and have five-star success in your personal and professional endeavors, you must want to win and want to win badly. You must develop a five-star mindset and a winner's attitude. You must develop the will to win! As Vince Lombardi said, "The difference between a successful person and others is not a lack of strength or knowledge, but rather a lack of the will to win!"

Book Recommendations and My Gift to You

When I first read *Think and Grow Rich* by Napoleon Hill, I couldn't put the book down. The only book I have read more often has been the Bible. Both inspired me and transformed my thinking and my perspective about success and achievement. I recommend you read both. Specifically, I want to recommend you get a copy of "The Message" version of the Bible by Eugene Peterson. It is not a direct translation from the original language, but it is a very motivational, up-to-date version of the Bible using contemporary language—no "thees" and "thous"!

I often think back to the friend who blessed me with a copy of *Think and Grow Rich*, since afterward I started reading one self-help book after another, simply because someone gave me a free copy of one great self-help book. I want to do the same for you. I want to give you some self-help books to get you growing and going! Go to www.williejolley.com/gift and get free digital copies of self-help books that blessed me, as well as books that I have written. Read them and share them, because they will positively impact you and also your friends and family. Remember, you want to uplift and empower the people who you hang around as well as yourself. Why? Because who you hang out with is who you will become, good or bad. If you hang with nine losers, you will probably become number ten, so if you want improved success, improve the success of your closest friends and family.

Are You Ready to Win?

Most people have the will to win, few are really ready to win and have the will to prepare to win.

—ICONIC BASKETBALL COACH JOHN WOODEN

Success vs. Winning

When I was working with the Washington, DC, public school system, we had an in-depth discussion one day over lunch about success. Some said, "Success is being happy," while others said, "Success is having a lot of money!" I sat and listened, but I was actually not sure what success was. I believed that money played a part, but there were people who hit the lottery and got millions, yet I also knew that statistics showed that most were unable to sustain the money over time and were unable to do it a second time. Then I thought about the "being happy" definition and thought about people I had met over the years who lived in small, modest homes and were very happy. So with those happy but not wealthy folks in mind, I didn't think that money in itself was enough to denote success.

So, I struggled with coming up with a good working definition. Then, some weeks later a friend gave me a copy of *Think and Grow Rich* by Napoleon Hill. As I read that book I realized that the definition of success that Hill learned from the many successful people he interviewed for the book was the most on-point definition. The book defined success as "the ongoing realization of a worthy goal or ideal!"

The more I thought about all the opinions that had been offered by my coworkers, and the more I counterbalanced their opinions with Napoleon Hill's definition, the more I realized that Napoleon Hill was onto something. I thought about the small-business person who was working hard every day and growing his or her business and positively impacting their community. That person was a success because they were seeing the ongoing realization of a worthy goal and ideal. Or how about the dad and mom working hard to raise their children to be valuable members of society. Even though they are not wealthy, they are able to send all their children to college and see them graduate and go on to become positive members of society. Those parents are a success. They were seeing the ongoing realization of a worthy goal or ideal.

Yet, what about winning? How does success differ from winning? When we think of winning, we usually think about those who are first in a contest, but that is not the totality of winning. Winning is also about overcoming our own self-limiting beliefs and making a personal commitment to fight through the challenges in order to achieve a goal. Webster defines *winning* as

"To succeed or gain by exerting great effort!" It is like achieving; winning takes effort. It takes work!

Winning is not just about being the best or finishing first. It can also be about moving forward in the face of overwhelming odds. A person who runs a marathon without legs and finishes dead last is a winner. A single mom who decides to go back to school and get a college degree while still working a full-time job and raising her family is a winner—no matter how long it takes her to do it. The businessperson who hits a rough patch and goes deep into debt and loses all their savings, yet comes back, starts over, and turns a profit—that person is a winner! Winning is not just about finishing first.

It takes great effort to win in life. The reason most people do not win is because they are not willing to exert enough consistent effort. Many people sincerely go after a goal and work really hard at it for a while, but then they fall off, and eventually give up. As I have studied successful people over the years, I have been amazed by the similarities in those who consistently win. These successful people are not extraordinary personalities, but rather ordinary people who do extraordinary things and thus become extraordinary! They are people who start out after a goal and refuse to give up until they achieve that goal. They are the people who make up their minds that they are not going to stop. This is the key to their success—*they made up their minds.*

That's right, the first key to developing the winner's edge is a made-up mind!

Make Up Your Mind

Most people do not succeed in life because they do not make up their minds. They never make the commitment to win. What hinders most people in the quest for success is commitment. We talk about wanting to succeed and we think about success, but we don't jump in with everything we have within us. The great philosopher Johann Wolfgang von Goethe said:

> Until one is committed there is hesitance, the chance to draw back. Always ineffectiveness, concerning all acts of initiative and creation, there is one elemental truth the ignorance of which kills countless ideas and splendid plans; that the moment one commits oneself, then Providence [the hand of God] moves, too. All sorts of things occur to help that would never have otherwise occurred. A whole stream of events arise from the decision, raising in one's favor all manner of unforeseen incidents and meetings and material assistance which no man could have dreamed would come his way. Whatever you can do or dream you can do, begin it! Boldness has genius, power, and magic in it. Begin it now!

It takes that commitment to win, and that begins with a made-up mind. Make up your mind, commit yourself, and then get busy! This is how you get the will to win.

Winning takes a winner's mindset and a willingness to get past the circumstances and the challenges and keep going to achieve your goal. It takes work! If you are committed to excellence, then you can become unstoppable. People and circumstances might not help you to achieve your goal but ultimately you make the choice to either let "fate" win, or you will win. I encourage you to continue to pursue excellence and make the choice to win or to lose. It really is your choice.

It's All About Your Attitude

Those who expect to win, tend to win more than those who don't. In my music CD, entitled *Money Making Music and Motivation*, the song called "It's All About Your Attitude"[1] highlights the fact that everything really is all about your attitude! Let me close part one with some of the lyrics to that song:

First Verse
ATTITUDE . . . One small eight-letter word, yet it has such
    a big impact on your success or on your failure.
Attitude is not just about a disposition, but also about
    how you see the world. It's how you see life.
Do you see it from a negative perspective? Or do you
    see it from a positive perspective?
It's your choice! It's about your attitude . . . It's all about
    your attitude!

---

[1] "It's All About Your Attitude," words by Willie Jolley, music by Paul Minor. On the album *Money Making Music and Motivation*.

See my friend Keith Harrell wrote a book called *Attitude Is Everything.*

He was telling the truth . . . Attitude truly is everything!

It's about how you view things, how you perceive things, and how you go after things!

Can you control the time? No! Can you control the weather? No!

Can you control what other people say or do? No, No, No!

You can only control YOU and your attitude!

Your attitude to life determines your *altitude* in life! It's all about your attitude!

Second Verse

Now Dennis Brown says, "The only difference between a good day and a bad day is your attitude."

See, stuff is gonna happen. Life is gonna happen. Change is gonna happen.

Someone once said, "In life you either got a problem, you just left a problem, or you're on your way to a problem; that's life."

But you've got a choice. You've got a choice how you perceive and how you respond to life.

See, stuff happens to everyone. I wrote a book called *A Setback Is a Setup for a Comeback* . . . because that's all it is.

Setbacks happen to you, they happen to me, they happen to everybody.

But a setback is never the end of the road; it's a bend in the road,

And the only ones who crash are those who fail to make the turn.

It's about your attitude! It's all about your attitude.

Chorus:

It's about your attitude
It's about your attitude
It's about your attitude
It's all about your attitude

Third Verse

Now as you turn your setbacks into comebacks, you
    have got to make some decisions.
The first decision you got to make is to decide what do
    you do when you have a setback?
How do you see it, what's your perspective? Do you see
    it as a setback period, or as a setback comma?
Setback period means end of a sentence, no more to be
    said.
But a setback comma means pause, transition, more to
    come.
You see it from another perspective. And see if you see it
    another way, you'll start to be it from another way.
See, you must understand that you must make some
    tough decisions.
Because you can't control what happens to you, you
    can't control what happens around you, but you've
    got complete control over what happens in you!
And you can choose to be happy! That's your choice!
So choose to have a positive attitude.
Next you must make a decision to stay away from
    negative people,
Negative, small-minded, petty-thinking people who tell
    you what's not possible for your life. You must make
    a commitment to stay away from them.
Some of them are going to be in your innercircle. People
    who you love and they love you, too. They're not

trying to be mean-spirited, they just happen to suffer
from possibility blindness!

No, you've got to make a commitment to stay away from
negative people and live your dreams!

See, folks, you must make a commitment to work on
you. If you take a grapefruit and squeeze it, what are
you going to get? Grapefruit juice!

If you take an orange and squeeze it, what are you going
to get? Orange juice!

If you take a negative person and squeeze them, what
are you going to get?

That's right—negative!

You must make a commitment to fill yourself with the
pure, the positive, and the powerful! Because your
input determines your output!

It's all about your attitude! It's all about your attitude!

Conclusion

We are nearing the end of part one of this book. So far we have
looked closely at the five secrets to having a five-star organization:

1. Develop the leader within. Remember, before you can lead many,
   you must be able to lead yourself.

2. See change as an ally, not as an enemy. Change happens to us all;
   it is ongoing and never ending. If you understand the components
   of change, challenge, and choices, you will learn to succeed as you
   grow through the changes, not just *go* through them.

3. Develop a team that learns to think like a team and work like a
   team, so you can win like a team. Keep in mind that great teams
   care for each other, cover for each other, and encourage each

other. If you can do this, you will see that five-star success is not just for a select few but possible for every organization and every person in the organizations.

4. Embrace great customer service. Learn to live the ten commandments of Superior Customer Service. Service is the rent we pay for living on this earth. The more we serve, the more success we will have and the more our lives will be fulfilled.

5. Develop a positive attitude and organizational atmosphere. Change and setbacks are going to happen whether we like it or not, so those who accept the principle that change is good when your attitude is great, succeed more often and enjoy the process more often. Those places that embrace and encourage a positive atmosphere are the organizations that will have happy people who come to work every day ready to go the extra mile to help the organization to win!

We have looked at having the will to win and the determination to always get better, to have an unending pursuit of better. Are you ready to commit to being better? It takes a daily commitment, and that's why I have made a point to remind myself on a daily basis about the importance of getting better each and every day. Whether in business or in life, it is critical to work on getting better and that starts with working on yourself.

In the marriage book I wrote with my wife, *Make Love, Make Money, Make It Last,* we wrote the following: "If you want a better marriage and better relationship, you must work on becoming a better partner. If you want better children, you must continue to become a better parent, and if you want a better life, you must continue to become a better you!" The concept is built on the premise that we can wish for an easier path, we can pray that God moves all of our mountains, or we can work on ourselves to get better and conquer the mountains as they appear in the way.

My friend Zemira Jones, one of America's top management experts, often tells me, "The harder we are on ourselves, the easier life tends to be on us. Yet the easier we are on ourselves, the harder life is on us!" Given this, you see how it is crucial to make the commitment to work hard on yourself. In fact, it should be a top priority. Jim Rohn, the great business philosopher, said, "Learn to work harder on yourself than you do on your job. If you work hard on your job you can make a living, but if you work hard on yourself you'll make a fortune." In other words, if you work harder on yourself than on anything else, you will find your success will increase in every part of your life.

PART TWO

The Five Simple Steps for Your Personal Five-Star Success

If a man is called to be a street sweeper, he should sweep streets even as Michelangelo painted, or Beethoven composed music, or Shakespeare wrote poetry. He should sweep streets so well that all the hosts of heaven and earth will pause to say, here lived a great street sweeper who did his job well!

—Martin Luther King, Jr. Memorial, Washington, DC

Pursuing Your
Personal Success

A man can be as great as he wants to be. If you believe in yourself and have the courage, the determination, the dedication, the competitive drive, and if you are willing to sacrifice the little things in life and pay the price for the things that are worthwhile, it can be done.

—VINCE LOMBARDI

The second half of this book is the second part of a two-part process to create extraordinary results, both personal and professional. While part one focused on secrets for developing a five-star culture of excellence, ones used by outstanding organizations and ones you could apply to help you grow professionally, part two is designed to help you develop your personal power and your personal potential and possibilities. Your personal power positively or negatively impacts the success of the organizations that you are involved with, because it impacts you and you are a vital part of the organization (everyone who works at an organization is vital because the chain is only as strong as the weakest link). Plus, your personal power also plays a tremendous role in whether you personally succeed, or don't.

Part two looks at specific things you need to do in order to achieve personal success. If you follow the five steps in this part of the book, it will have a positive impact on your life and your personal success and achievement. The results that you will be able to achieve personally can help you and your family, your business, and your future. The best part about these steps is that they are not mysterious, nor do they comprise a mystifying formula. In fact, you probably have some familiarity with some of these steps. You just need to be shown a different perspective. In these five steps you'll see the importance of several things:

1. Have vision for your life. Focus on what's positively possible rather than a seemingly probable negative result.
2. Figure out what you want from life and how badly you want it.
3. Confront your failures and self-limiting behaviors.
4. Get excited and engaged with what's in front of you now.
5. Master the art of leading self.
6. Learn not to settle for mediocrity but continually strive for excellence day in and day out.

You don't need to be a rocket scientist or a nuclear physicist to understand these steps. I learned years ago that the most effective messaging is first of all simple, eighth-grade-level communication, and second, communication that is direct and to the point. So, I present these steps to you in a truly simple way so you can use them to set your life on a trajectory toward success. If you apply them, you will see substantial results in a short time. That last part is important: You must apply them in order to see results.

The Path to Personal Excellence

Many people speak about how they are waiting for their ship to come in. They patiently sit and wait for their break to come. I used to do the same thing. During my days as a nightclub performer (before the days of *American Idol*), I was always waiting for my "Big Break," waiting to get discovered. (I didn't realize that most of the people in the nightclub were too drunk to discover their way out the front door.)

I had always heard people say, "Just keep singing, sing real hard, and one day somebody will give you a break!" I kept waiting for my break, but it never came. Then I learned to stop *waiting* for my break and start *making* my breaks. I learned that success is a choice that you must make happen, not a chance that you sit and wait for. I love the old Chinese proverb that states, "He who waits for roasted duck to fly into his mouth, waits a very, very long time!"

I decided that the best way to grow my future was to first grow myself. So, I started a program of self-development. I decided that I was no longer going to wait for my breaks. I was going to make my breaks. I was going to follow the advice of comedian Jonathan Winters. He said, "I kept waiting for success, but it didn't come, so I just went on without it."

Got Your Swim Gear Ready?

When I was at a crossroad in my life, I realized I had a choice that I needed to make: I could continue to wait for my ship to come in or I could swim out to it. I decided to swim out to it, and I am so glad I did because some of my friends are still standing at the pier, waiting. You see, success is not a thing to be waited for—it is a thing to be achieved! You should not wait for your ship to come in. Jump in and start swimming to it! Make a commitment to be proactive about your success. Make a commitment to take action today on your dreams and goals. Decide now that your personal success is worth the work.

Are you ready to start taking the steps to get there? If so, let's get it on!

Wake Up and Dream!
Wake Up the Winner Within
. . . So You Can Dream!

We all have ideas that pop into our heads that could literally transform our lives, yet most people disregard or ignore these ideas. I like to ask people in my programs this question: "How many of you have had at least one good idea in your lives?" Most people raise their hands. Then I ask, "How many of you have talked yourself out of one good idea?" And again, most people raise their hands. Finally, I ask, "How many of you have had an idea that you knew was a good idea, you thought about it, yet you didn't move on it, and a year or two later you saw someone else living your idea?" Again, most of the hands go up! Typically, we think about the idea, but we do not move on it, because we have not sold ourselves on the idea. How would life be different if we took action on our ideas?

Many people are just going through the motions of life; they behave like robots. They get up, go to work, come home, watch television, and go to bed. A friend of mine, the late, great speaker author John Alston, used to share in his speeches as he stepped from side to side, backward and forward on a stage: "Most people get up (step up), go to work (step to the side), come home (step back), and go to bed (step to the other side)." Of course, if they are working parents, they typically have an additional step: They get up, go to work, come home, then again go to work, and then go to bed!

Most people have a routine that ends each day back where they started. Day in and day out, they do the same thing and consistently get the same results week in and week out. Some have described this behavior as a form of sleepwalking or like walking on a treadmill—the person is moving but not really going anywhere. They are in a state of merely existing or surviving, when they should be in a state of thriving! They have not woken up to the possibilities for their lives. We must wake up. We must wake up mentally and think differently!

Dorothea Brand wrote a book called *Wake Up and Live* in which she extolled the virtues of looking at life through different lenses. She said, "We need to realize that there are incredible opportunities and possibilities all around, within our grasp if we would just wake up and live!"

You must make the commitment to live life to the fullest and take advantage of all the wonderful things life has to offer you. Those who make the commitment to success realize that they can, and should, live life to the fullest. And that they should do it *now*.

Frank Sinatra once said, "You should live your life full out, like it is your last day—because one day you will be right!" My godmother, Rosita Perez, the late, great speaker, liked to put it this way, "Don't take our music with you to the grave. Live full, die empty!"

Unfortunately, most people do not live life to the fullest. They want more out of life, but they are not willing to put more into life. They live their lives sitting in front of a fireplace saying, "Give me heat," without adding any wood, and without even starting a fire! Far too often we live life like the sports teams that are so afraid to lose, they never try to win.

Are You Sleepwalking Through Life?

If we aren't willing to put forth the effort, we are settling for mediocrity. If we blindly go with the flow of those around us, we are sleepwalking, not fully living. If we are not careful in choosing those we follow, we can follow the wrong leader, someone who is not taking us where we need to go. In the 1950s, radio host and success coach Earl Nightingale recorded the landmark self-help program *The Strangest Secret*. He stated that most people are doomed to failure because they are like robots in the process of following the leader. Unfortunately, the leaders they are following don't know where they are going, and it becomes a hopeless game of the blind leading the blind! He quoted the noted psychiatrist Rollo May, by stating the "opposite of courage is not cowardice, it is conformity."

Nightingale also said, "Less than 5 percent of Americans are wealthy . . . in the wealthiest country in the world. Most people today are living a life of conformity, where they conform to the populace. Unfortunately, the populace is going in the wrong direction."

This is evident in America today, one of the richest countries the world has ever seen. Yet many people in America are not able to take advantage of the great opportunities that are available. Statistics show that people from other countries become millionaires five times faster in America than those who are born here. Why? Because they may come from a country where they make ten dollars a day and then they come to America and realize they can make ten dollars an hour! They get busy. They come and live the American dream, achieving it before those who are born here realize there is an American dream! I can attest to the fact that the American dream is alive and well, but you must first be willing to dream, then pursue that dream and work to make it a reality!

Knowing What You Want

I believe that in order to succeed and win more, we have to confront our fears and self-limiting behaviors. I have learned that we must have honest conversations with ourselves.

I encourage you to ask yourself the following questions in this order:

1. What do I want?
2. What am I doing to get what I want?
3. What more could I be doing to get what I want?
4. What must I stop doing to get what I want?

You can answer this set of questions for each thing you want. For example, if my answer to the first question is that I want to lose weight, then perhaps my answer to the second question might be that I am presently working out four times a week. Then I would think about what else I could do. So the next answer might be to add another day of exercise each week, or to eat more fruits and vegetables. Then I would need to answer the final question, the one I call "the ouch question"—what must I stop doing in order to get what I want? The answer might be to stop eating dinner late at night. Or to stop eating fried foods every day at lunch. Or to stop having a bowl of ice cream as a treat at night.

I encourage you to have an honest conversation with yourself and answer these questions. I also encourage you to continue to work on thinking big and playing big. And make the commitment to tell yourself daily to stop playing small!

After You Wake Up . . . Dream!

Wake up and *then* dream? You might say this is an oxymoron. How do you dream while you're awake? This might sound strange, but in order to have success and live life to the fullest you must wake up—and then dream! By dream, I mean get a vision for your life. You must have a vision if you are going to live life to the fullest. I want you to grab your vision and see that this is a great time to be alive. You must catch the vision! Scripture says, "When there is no vision, the people perish!" (Proverbs 29:18, KJV). What goes unsaid is that when there *is* a vision, people can flourish!

Your vision is a critical component to living the five-star life and enjoying five-star success. It is hard to live life to the fullest if you haven't conceived what that kind of life would look like. If you do not have a vision in your mind, and you do not know where you are going, how can you ever achieve it? It is like the scene in *Alice's Adventures in Wonderland*. Alice came to a fork in the road, looked up in the tree, saw the smiling Cheshire cat, and asked the Cheshire cat which road she should take. The dialogue, paraphrased here, goes something like this:

The Cheshire cat inquired, "Where are you going?"

Alice replied, "I don't know!"

The Cheshire cat said, "In that case, any road will do!"

Most of us are like Alice; we are working hard, but sometimes we have no specific goal. In other words, we are going through life and when all is said and done we don't know where we are going.

In order to live life to the fullest, it is absolutely necessary that you start with your dreams. They are the seeds for success.

If you took a corn seed, dug a hole, planted it, and watered it, in time it would become a corn stalk. If you took an acorn and dug a hole and planted the acorn in the ground and watered it, in time it would become an oak tree. The same is true for your dreams.

If you can dream, and then you plant that dream in your heart and water it continually, in time, that dream can and will become a reality. But you need to know how to water the dream. You must water it by constantly saying, "I believe I can do it! I believe I can do it!" You must do this on good days and bad days, happy days and sad days, sunny days and rainy days. You must continue to affirm that your dreams can come true. If you do, then your dream will grow, blossom, and burst into being.

Visualizing Your Dreams

My dear friend and "brother from another mother" Al Walker—the great speaker and humorist—shared with me a lesson about the power of visualization from the movie *The Karate Kid*. In the film, a young man named Daniel had moved to a new area with his mother and was trying to fit in, yet he was having difficulty. One day, while going home from school on his bicycle, he was attacked by the local bullies who tore up his bicycle. They were ready to tear him up when out of nowhere a man who had martial arts skills came to his rescue and beat up the bullies, allowing Daniel to escape. This man was Mr. Miyagi, and he became Daniel's friend and mentor.

In one scene, Daniel was at Mr. Miyagi's home and he observed Mr. Miyagi carefully clipping a bonsai tree. Daniel was very impressed with the tree and asked Mr. Miyagi where he had learned such a fine art. Mr. Miyagi told Daniel that he had learned it from his father in Okinawa. Mr. Miyagi then told Daniel, "Come, you try."

Daniel proclaimed that he didn't know how. Mr. Miyagi encouraged Daniel to sit down anyway to try it, and again Daniel declined, stating that he "might mess it up." Mr. Miyagi told Daniel to close his eyes. "Trust," he said. Daniel closed his eyes. "Concentrate," Mr. Miyagi said. "Think only tree." He continued to tell Daniel to focus on the tree and see it in detail. He told him to clear his mind of everything but the tree. He asked Daniel if he had the image in his mind. Daniel nodded yes.

Finally, Mr. Miyagi asked Daniel to open his eyes. When Daniel opened his eyes, he saw that Mr. Miyagi had turned him away from the finished, clipped bonsai tree and toward an unfinished, unclipped bonsai tree. "Remember picture?" Mr. Miyagi asked him. Daniel said he did. Mr. Miyagi handed him clippers and told him to work on what he had seen in his mind. And Daniel did.

The moral of the story is that you cannot *be* what you cannot *see*. You must have a vision.

I say that you have to get excited about getting a vision for your life. Then get excited about all the wonderful opportunities and possibilities that are within your grasp. Get excited about the fact that you are still in the land of the living! Therefore, you have an opportunity to change your life for the better. In fact, you have an opportunity to live the absolute best life ever! Not only is it possible to change your life for the better, but those who are able to master this skill of being able to dream big dreams are those who have the greatest success. For years, I have shared with my audiences that dreams are the seed for success. I have illustrated this by giving examples of people who were willing to dream and how those dreams helped them achieve great success. Let's look at five lives that show just that.

King of the Court

When Michael Jordan was asked in an interview to describe the secret to his incredible success on the basketball court, he gave an answer that reveals the power of having vision. Michael Jordan didn't make his high school's varsity basketball team the first time he tried out. He went home and *started dreaming* about doing impossible things with a basketball, in order to prove to the coach that he had what it took.

Once Michael saw these incredible basketball exploits in his mind, he realized that he could do them on the court. So he went out on the court and replicated what he had dreamed about. He found that he could achieve those things that he dreamed about!

Michael continued dreaming, continued practicing, and continued to get better. He soon gained mastery over the ball, including developing his amazing dunking ability. He went on to be called "one of the greatest basketball players who ever lived." Among his many accomplishments were six NBA championships, being inducted into the Professional Basketball Hall of Fame, Olympic gold medalist (twice; once as an amateur while playing in college and again as a professional on America's "Dream Team"), and NBA's Most Valuable Player (five times while playing for the Chicago Bulls). He even had a pair of sneakers named after him: Nike's Air Jordans, the sales of which still provide the retired ball player with tens of millions of dollars a year.

Jazz Composer Extraordinaire

When accomplished musician Duke Ellington, winner of twelve Grammy Awards, was asked what the key to his success was, he responded, "I dreamed a lot!"

Duke Ellington grew up in Washington, DC, in a time where he had to struggle to build his music career. To support his music dream, he worked as a freelance sign painter and as a messenger for the U.S. Department of the Navy. When people would ask for him to paint a sign for their parties, he would ask if they had a band; if they didn't, he would volunteer. He would play piano at small parties and weddings on weekends and would write songs whenever he could catch a few minutes. He went to New York to try and be a part of the hot jazz scene there, but found it hard to crack, and eventually came back to DC.

Yet, he continued to dream about having an orchestra and being a successful musician. He kept dreaming and kept working on his dream, and eventually he got an opportunity to audition for a club in Atlantic City. He got the job. After a short time, people started filling up the club to catch this hot new combo. The word about the band reached the Cotton Club in New York and they just happened to be looking for a small orchestra to be their house band. Ellington organized a group of musicians and auditioned and got the job. They went on to become the hottest orchestra in New York. In time, Ellington recorded his songs and they became worldwide hits. You likely are familiar with one of his catchiest tunes, "It Don't Mean a Thing (If It Ain't Got That Swing)." He earned a Grammy Lifetime Achievement Award and was awarded posthumously the Pulitzer Prize in Music.

And it all began with a dream. He dreamed the dream, held on to that dream, and eventually became one of the greatest jazz musicians in the world. He said that the secret was that he kept on dreaming!

The Man Behind the World's Most Famous Mouse

Entrepreneur and animated film genius Walt Disney went from being bankrupt and suffering two nervous breakdowns to creating beloved cartoon characters and films that would lay the groundwork for an entertainment empire. He won multiple Oscars and became a multimillionaire. When he was asked how he was able to achieve this amazing transformation, he responded, "I kept on dreaming!"

And one of the most interesting things about his dream is that it continued even after his death. Even though his name is part of the official name, Walt Disney didn't see the opening of Walt Disney World Resort; however, he envisioned it. The story goes that after Walt Disney opened Disneyland in California and it became the number-one tourist attraction in America, he started working on his next dream: a bigger, grander version of the theme park, this one on the opposite side of the country. He bought swampland in a little sleepy town called Orlando, Florida, and commenced work on his big dream. Construction was going great, but then Walt got sick. He was diagnosed with lung cancer, and he died within a year. The construction continued and some years later Disney World opened. It was spectacular.

On opening day a lady came up to Roy Disney, Walt's brother, and said, "Isn't it sad that Walt didn't get to see this?" Roy said, "Sad? No! It's because Walt had the dream and saw it, that it's here today!"

Champion-Sized Dreams

Muhammad Ali was once asked how he revolutionized the boxing industry so that people would flock to see him box. He answered, "I had a dream and used my imagination and created a personality that people either loved or they hated! Those who loved me came to see me win! Those who hated me came to see me lose. In the meantime, every seat was taken!"

This world heavyweight champion and boxing gold medalist also used his imagination to dream big dreams for himself. In his memoir, *The Soul of a Butterfly: Reflections on a Life Journey*, he shared a quote that inspired him: "If my mind can conceive it, and my heart can believe it—then I can achieve it."

Believing Without Seeing

Helen Keller, a well-known American author whose story has been told in print and on film, was blind and deaf from infancy in a time when people who were deaf and blind were often committed to institutions. Her circumstances did not limit her imagination. She had a dream to become great, and she worked diligently on achieving her dream. Through the persistence, encouragement, and mentorship of her teacher Anne Sullivan, coupled with Helen's own perseverance and desire to achieve, she not only learned to communicate effectively using sign language and braille, she also became the first blind and deaf student to graduate from college. She went on to become one of the greatest people the world has ever seen.

Helen Keller was asked once in an interview, "Is there anything worse than blindness?" Her answer was, "Yes, having sight but no vision!"

• • •

All of these successful people had a vision. They saw their dreams and then they made them happen. Albert Einstein said it so aptly when he declared, "Imagination, the power to dream, is much more important than knowledge." Those who have the greatest success are those who are able to dream the greatest dreams!

Keep Dreaming, Even When There's Opposition

Many people downplay the importance of dreaming because at some time in their lives they have been cautioned by a "caring" friend or loved one to stop dreaming and get real. I say "caring" friend or loved one with tongue in cheek, because many of the people who kill our dreams are not enemies or foes, but friends and loved ones who are not trying to be mean-spirited. They just suffer from possibility blindness!

In my book *It Only Takes a Minute to Change Your Life*, there is a wonderful soliloquy about how we often think that the most dangerous people are only those who hit us with clubs or shoot us with guns, but in reality some of the most dangerous people are people who knock down our hopes and dreams and shoot holes in our ideas. I often quote it on my radio show. Feel free to go to www.attitudeofexcellence.com/poem to listen and get inspired for yourself!

Don't Just Dream at Night

The importance of the concept of waking up and dreaming became evident when I was about to release my second book, *A Setback Is a Setup for a Comeback*. The text was at the publishing company. I had checked the proofs. It was about to go to the printer when a friend sent me a quote that was so profound I had to have it in the book. I read the quote and immediately picked up the phone and called my publisher. "Please, stop the presses!" I said. "I have something that has to go in the book!"

I am so glad the publisher accepted the addition. I was really inspired by the quote and so were thousands of others who have commented in person or via email. The quote, from T.E. Lawrence, who was also known as Lawrence of Arabia, was: "Some people dream at night in the dusty recesses of their minds and when they awake they awake to find that it was just vanity. But those people who dream with their eyes open are the dangerous ones, because they dream with their eyes open and they make their dreams come true!"

Not only must you start dreaming, you must continue to dream and keep dreaming big! Studies show that people with dreams and goals live longer than those who don't have them. You have got to have a dream! The bigger the dream, the bigger the rewards. Most people go through life never realizing the great potential and possibilities that lie within themselves. Ralph Waldo Emerson said, "What lies behind us and what lies before us are tiny matters compared to what lies within us." We live in a time of unlimited opportunities and possibilities, yet so many of us sleep through life. If we don't wake up, we won't recognize the greatness that is within us.

• • •

My questions to you are: What is the vision you have in your mind for your life? What is your dream? If you had a magic wand and could tap your life and have it become what you wanted, what would it be? What do you see? How does it look? Can you see the detail? Remember, scripture teaches that without a vision, people will perish. And I add, yet with a vision, people will flourish. What do you see for yourself in a year? Five years? Ten years? If you can't see it, how will you ever be it? Will you make a commitment to wake up and dream?

Show Up!
Show Up with Your Stuff

The next step necessary to living life to the fullest and having five-star success is that you must show up! That means you need to show up excited, show up enthusiastic, show up engaged, and show up determined to demonstrate excellence. You must show up and then go further than you are expected to go, do more than you are expected to do, and give more than you are expected to give.

I recommend you do more than you are paid to do because it can have a big impact on your future income. I have learned over many years of speaking and training, that if you do more than you are paid to do, one day you will be paid more for what you do normally. I love the quote that Les Brown, the Motivator, uses. He said, "If you do the things today that others won't do, you will have the things tomorrow that others won't have!" That is why you must show up daily and consistently perform with an attitude of excellence.

It has been said that 80 percent of success is simply showing up—and I believe that saying is absolutely right! I learned a lesson that supports this concept of the impact of simply showing up. Early in my speaking career, Les Brown was scheduled to speak at an event in Washington, DC. He was walking down the hall at the hotel on his way to the ballroom before his evening keynote speech and he heard me speak at a small conference. He came in after hearing me speak and mentioned that he was about to launch a tour called the Music and Motivation Tour, and needed an opening act who could speak and sing. He offered me the opportunity and I quickly accepted. Not long after that we were on the tour, which featured Les Brown, iconic singer Gladys Knight, and great organist and singer Billy Preston.

One night while waiting for the show to begin, I was in the green room with Les and Gladys, flipping through channels on the television. I saw a face I knew on the screen. The lady was on television selling tapes on "how to have a successful marriage." She was calling herself "a relationship expert." My mouth dropped open. I asked, "How in the world can she talk about relationships? I know that lady! She's been married five times!" Les laughed and said, "Willie, the reason she is there is because she showed up!" And Les was right. I knew people who were more qualified to talk about marriage than she was, but they didn't show up. People who have had lasting and loving relationships did not show up; she did!

I learned that you must make the commitment to show up and move in the direction of your dreams and goals. Once you show up, make the commitment to continue to keep showing up! Show up and take it to the next level—on a daily basis! Show up excited about your job or whatever tasks you are expected to perform. Make a commitment to your commitment and keep showing up.

Many people do not succeed in life, not because they do not have the talent or the ability to do great things, but because they simply do not decide to show up. They don't show up and let the world know that they are there and have something to say.

Here is what my friend Dr. Dennis Kimbro says happens when you show up:

- If you simply *show up* . . . you get the business and opportunities, 80 percent of the time.
- If you show up *on time* . . . you get the business and opportunities 85 percent of the time.
- If you show up on time *with a plan* . . . you get the business and opportunities 90 percent of the time.
- If you show up on time, with a plan, *and implement that plan* . . . you get the business and opportunities 95 percent of the time.

- If you show up on time, with a plan, and implement that plan with excellence . . . you get the business and opportunities almost 100 percent of the time!

I wish I could say you get the opportunities 100 percent of the time if you do everything right, but I can't. Yet, I *can* say that when you do the right things and perform with a spirit of excellence, your winning ratio goes up exponentially! I recommend you make a commitment to show up on time and with a plan, and then execute your plan with excellence!

Leaning on Your Network

I learned about showing up and pursuing excellence when I got an opportunity to do a show on Sirius XM. I was told they didn't have a big budget or money for a producer. I decided to show up and do the best I could and try to make something positive happen despite the limited budget.

Since I didn't have much money to work with, I decided to work with what I did have, and that was a lot of good friends. I called friends and asked them if they would do me a favor and be on my radio show. I told them the challenges and told them I would appreciate their help in launching this new show. Each one I asked said, "Yes!" One lesson I have learned over the years is that most people want to help and they will help, if you ask and give them a reason as to why their assistance can make a big difference.

So I started doing interviews with my friends, people I had met over the years at speaking industry events. I interviewed Les Brown, the Motivator; the well-known cookie man Wally "Famous" Amos; Sheryl Lee Ralph from the Broadway hit *Dreamgirls*; sales and goal-setting expert Brian Tracy; business icon Nido Qubein; Mark Victor Hansen and Jack Canfield, the authors of the Chicken Soup for the Soul book series; and the inspirational motivational speaker W. Mitchell. From those friends I started meeting even more people who would become friends, such as iconic statesman General Colin Powell; hotel magnate Bill Marriott; leadership guru John Maxwell; sports leadership icon Coach Tony Dungy and CBS sports anchor James Brown; Daymond John from *Shark Tank*; gospel icons Marvin Winans and Bebe Winans, and Sheila Johnson, who is owner of the Washington Mystics basketball team. Sheila introduced me to Ted Leonis, the former AOL executive who is the owner of the Washington Wizards basketball team and the Washington Capitals hockey team.

Even though I didn't have a big budget, I learned the power of a great network, and the power of asking for help. As I was told once, "Asking for help doesn't make you weak; it helps to make and then keep you strong!" With the help of my friends, and a commitment to create excellent programming, I was able to build a radio show that became one of the top self-help/motivational shows in America. The key was that I was willing to show up and do the best I could with what I had to work with. The show led to a popular podcast called The Willie Jolley Wealthy Ways podcast. So you can listen to the show on Sirius XM or listen to the podcast and get inspired by some of the greatest thinkers in the world—go on iTunes or iHeartMedia and listen whenever you like!

I encourage you to continue to show up and be counted, and when you are counted, be counted with a spirit of excellence!

The Price for Success

When I was starting out in the speaking business, I was struggling with growing my business. I was only charging about a hundred dollars per speech and struggling to get that. I kept hearing of a success coach who was helping people to rapidly grow their businesses and I decided to call his office and learn how I could go to one of his events.

I spoke with his assistant and asked her if it was true what I had been hearing, and she confirmed that it was true: He was absolutely sharing principles that helped people to rapidly grow their businesses. She told me that his events were three-day events and that he only had a couple per year. I asked when the next event was planned for, and she told me that there was only one left for the year and there was only one seat left for that event. I quickly shouted out, "That is my seat! I am supposed to be there!" Then I asked her what was the cost of the event and she said, "Ten thousand dollars!" I gulped and said, "Did you say ten thousand dollars?" I asked her to repeat herself and she repeated the same figure. My small thinking kicked in and I wondered, "Heck, she must be kidding! Ten thousand dollars for three days? I will stay home and figure it out myself!"

Yet, a wiser voice came to my mind, a voice that reminded me that I had to pay for college and had to pay for graduate school, and reminded me that there is a price for success. In addition to the fact that there is a price for success, there is also a cost for not paying the price. There is a cost for college and graduate school. There is a cost to become a master craftsman or trade specialist. There is a cost for law school, medical school, or dental school. There is a cost for excellence! I thought about my boyhood friends who chose not to attend classes in high school and chose not to go on for more training and learning after high school, and how many of them were still in the same place they were twenty years ago. There's the cost of wasting time and staying in the same place year after year.

I realized that I did not want to be in the same place the following year as I was in at that moment, so I told the lady on the phone that I was coming and would send a small deposit immediately and get the rest to her soon. I hung up the phone and sent her a check for the few hundred dollars I had in my bank account. Then I went to work on raising that money. I didn't steal, but I certainly did beg and borrow, and I raised the money and confirmed my seat. I went to that three-day event and it changed my thinking and changed my business. I came back home and went to work on the principles I had learned and quickly made enough money to pay back all the people I had borrowed and begged money from, plus money in the bank for growing my business.

The next year when he had his seminar I not only went back but also took my wife, but this time I didn't have to beg or borrow; I simply wrote a check! I learned that there is a price for success and then there is a cost for not paying the price.

Great achievements always have a price. There is a price for education and there is a price you must pay for developing yourself to be all you can be. There is a price for pushing past your comfort level, to sweat and toil to reach your goals. There is a price in terms of having to invest in yourself and in your personal development. There is a price for you to have to give up some of the comforts or conveniences others might enjoy, when you have to read, and study, and work on your abilities in any discipline. In other words, there is a price for excellence and there is a price for all achievements. I recommend you pay the price to become excellent. And I recommend you make a commitment to not waste time. You can always make more money, but you cannot make more time. So you cannot afford to waste time. Once it is gone, it cannot be reclaimed. Take full advantage of the time you have, because it is not guaranteed!

Keep Showing Up, Even When
Others Knock You Down

I had an experience that made me realize that people do not always like the concept of excellence, especially when they are comfortable with mediocrity. I was scheduled to do a special event, my one-man music-and-motivation show at a national entrepreneurs' networking conference. My show was scheduled for the end of the evening on the second day, and I was looking forward to creating a memorable experience for the attendees. My one-man show is a unique experience for audience members because it offers a new way of mixing music and speaking with multimedia and high-tech visuals. It is a very complicated technological experience with different musical and video cues throughout the show. I was traveling that week, so my team sent the production crew my technical program in advance, so they could load it into their software and have access to it in advance. Due to my schedule I was not able to get to the facility until the morning of the day when I would perform the show that night. That morning when I went to the production director to get the time for the technical rehearsal, they told me they couldn't find the file we had sent. I told them no problem, I always carried an extra copy just for times when there was a problem. They said they couldn't do the rehearsal at that time but would let me know when they would be able to fit one in.

For the rest of the morning, then all afternoon and into the early evening, I asked for a technical rehearsal, and they continued to say, "We'll get to it later!" Finally, about two hours before show time I told them it was getting late and we really needed to get it done soon because it would probably take more time than they expected. They said no, we'll do it later. I told them this was not demonstrating excellence and we needed to get the rehearsal done now. I was told they felt they could wing it and if I had to have the rehearsal, the best they were willing to do was fifteen minutes before the show was scheduled to start. What? That was not enough time to go through all the slides and videos and make sure everything would be excellent! I shared that this was a highly technical presentation and we would need more time to make sure everything worked correctly. The more I talked, the more they resisted. In fact, after expressing again how this was not acceptable, I was told that I was "a pain"! Therefore, they decided that they would not do a rehearsal at all, and when I told them that was an example of mediocrity at the highest level, they decided to add insult to injury. They told me that because I kept "pestering them," they would not support my program and therefore I would not get any technical support, not even be given a microphone!

I could not believe my ears. The event manager said she had signed their contract and there was a clause for them to refuse to work with people they deemed as "problematic," so she recommended I cancel the show. She said it would be "impossible" to do it without a microphone. But, I shared that I would not cancel. I told her that the show was sold out and those people were going to get a show, with or without the production crew's support. I told her excellence never lets mediocrity win!

I went out that evening and started by coming on stage and sharing with the audience the predicament and the challenge. I shared that they had come for a show, and they were going to get one. So, for the next ninety minutes, I spoke, sang a cappella, and gave them the full show, with no visuals or technical reinforcements and no microphone. At the end of the night I got one of the longest, and loudest, standing ovations I have ever gotten in my career. People refused to stop clapping! And afterward I got some of the nicest notes I have ever gotten. One of them was life changing for me. Here is what it said:

> Dear Dr. Willie Jolley and Staff:
> I attended the Dr. Jolley's "Night to Change Your Life" One Man Music and Motivation Show at the entrepreneurs' networking conference in Maryland. I was amazed and have since started following Dr. Jolley on the Internet every day. Dr. Jolley's performance that night was one of the most powerful and incredible experiences I have ever personally witnessed. What stood out most was how he handled the "No Sound Support" situation from the sound company. He refused to quit and went on to deliver a wonderful show, but most of all he showed us firsthand how to handle adversity with grace. It was excellent! I learned more from that one incident than any book I could have read. I learned more about faith than any sermon could have

hoped to have conveyed. I saw the man that I want to be most like standing on that stage. I have nothing against Michael Jordan. But it's not MJ that I want to be like—it's Willie Jolley that I want to be most like. Thank You!
　　—Forrest Lamb

What I learned that night was that there is a price for excellence and that many will be intimidated when you want to pursue excellence, but don't let them stop you. Pursue excellence every day, in every way! Albert Einstein was right when he said, "Great spirits have always encountered violent opposition from mediocre minds!" I encourage you to pay the price and always pursue excellence! Show up and be excellent every day!

I love this quote by President Theodore Roosevelt, delivered in 1910 at the Sorbonne in Paris. It aptly describes how you must continue to be committed to your goals:

It is not the critic who counts; not the man who points out how the strong man stumbled, or where the doer of deeds could have done them better. The credit belongs to the man who is actually in the arena, whose face is marred by dust and sweat and blood; who strives valiantly; who errs and comes short again and again . . . ; who knows the great enthusiasms, the great devotions; who spends himself in a worthy cause; who, at the best, knows in the end the triumph of high achievement, and who, at the worst, if he fails, at least fails while daring greatly, so that his place shall never be with those timid souls who know neither victory nor defeat.

People may well talk about you and try to demean you because you choose to stick to your pursuit of excellence. They might make fun of you because you are going the extra mile and are not satisfied with mediocrity. They may ridicule you; yet, the result is well worth the price. Always show up, and show up with excellence!

Stand Up!

Develop the Leader Within

In this chapter, we're going to look at the importance of being able to lead yourself. There is power in realizing your leadership potential. There is an Arabian proverb I quoted in *A Setback Is a Setup for a Comeback* that applies here:

> He who knows not and knows not that he knows not, but thinks he knows . . . is a fool! Leave him alone!
>
> He who knows not and knows that he knows not is a child . . . teach him!
>
> Now, he who knows, yet knows not that he knows, is asleep . . . wake him.
>
> Oh, but he who knows, and knows that he knows, and uses what he knows, is a leader . . . follow him!

Commit to Always Getting Better

If you want to have greater success at work and at home, you must make the commitment to become a more effective leader of self, because before you can lead many, you must lead self. In order to achieve that goal, you have got to stand up on the inside and make the commitment to get better, do better, and be better.

In order to experience five-star success, we must be willing to get better in both our personal and professional pursuits. If we want better results in life, we must become a better you, and better at what we do, and we need to make the commitment to continue to improve on a daily basis. You've got to make a commitment to get better! I have come to the clear realization that when I started working on myself and working on getting better, life started getting better!

I was fortunate to hear an interview with Coach John Wooden, the legendary collegiate basketball coach of the UCLA Bruins, who won more collegiate championships than any other coach. Coach Wooden was in his midnineties when the interview was recorded. He was asked, "Coach, what are you doing every day in your retirement?" A second question was also asked: "Please tell us what was the secret to your winning so many championships during your time as the coach of the UCLA Bruins?" He responded by saying that he would answer both questions with one answer. "The secret to my success," he said, "is the secret to my life and is what I have been doing for the last sixty-five years and I continue to do now, each and every day: I work on me! I work on getting better!"

Coach Wooden said that as a young man, he made a commitment to become a lifelong learner and lifelong student of self-development. He discovered that those who have the greatest results over the long term are those who make a commitment to constantly improve themselves. And that those who constantly work on developing themselves will also develop their performance and accomplish more in life. Typically, those who have the greatest achievements are those who make a commitment to continually get better, each and every day! Just like the old chant goes: "I am getting better, each and every day, in each and every way!"

It was because of Coach Wooden's commitment to self-development that he never became satisfied with success and always tried to improve himself and his performance as a coach. He instilled this philosophy in his players and taught them that no matter who they played against, their biggest opponent was always themselves. He told them the tendency is to become satisfied with success; and therefore, in time, to create a pathway to mediocrity. Once his players caught on to his way of thinking, they consistently played at another level and consistently continued to improve their performance. That is why Coach Wooden won more college championships than any other coach in history.

For Coach Wooden it was all about constant and never-ending improvement. In the very same way, five-star organizations never become satisfied with success. They are always working on improving themselves and their performance, and you must do the same with yourself. Pat Riley, who is one of the most successful coaches in pro basketball, said it like this: "Excellence is the gradual result of always striving to do better! Doing a little more every day than you think you can!" Experience has taught me that Pat Riley and Coach Wooden were right: I discovered that the more I worked on myself, the more I achieved. Plus, the more I learned, the more I earned!

In your quest to get better, I encourage you to pursue the 1 percent solution; namely, to strive to get a little better each and every day. You need not make monumental improvements to get better results; you just need to be consistent and make the commitment to continue to work on getting incrementally better. If you are a little bit better than your competition, you can benefit in incredible ways. If you look at two horses in the Kentucky Derby who are running neck and neck toward the finish line, and one horse wins by a nose, that horse was a little better, and therefore got a winner's purse that was two to three times greater than the second place. Strive to get better consistently and you will see greater results!

Have the Courage to Stand Up and Be Counted

To become a leader of one, you must be willing to stand up and be counted. In order to win in life, you must stand up and face the challenges life presents with a determined spirit and a committed mind. I am not talking about physically standing up, but standing up on the inside. I have friends who are in wheelchairs and unable to physically stand up, yet they are taking life on and they courageously stand up on the inside.

My friend Art Berg, the late speaker and founder of e-Speakers (the revolutionary online calendar and back-office support system), was paralyzed in an automobile accident as a young man, but that did not keep him from success. He went on to accomplish incredible things with his life. He was named the Young Entrepreneur of the Year by the Small Business Administration and was named as one of the Success website's "American Comebacks."

Even though he was in a wheelchair, Art consistently stood up on the inside and faced his challenges with courage and a commitment to excellence. (I recommend you get a copy of his last book, *The Impossible Just Takes a Little Longer*. It will inspire you.) He believed that fate is the hand that you're dealt, but destiny is how you play that hand!

Stand up on the inside and face your problems and your challenges with a determined spirit and a committed mind.

Coach Tony Dungy was a guest on my Sirius XM show and shared a few unique thoughts on how winners stand out from everyone else. He said, "To win consistently you must embrace the critical E's of champions—Exceptional Expectations, Excellent Execution, and No Excuses!" He noted that excuses are the tools of the incompetent and that those who excel at them rarely excel at anything else. If we are going to be all we have the potential to be, we must stand up and be counted—and that takes courage. Courage is by definition the moral, mental, and spiritual strength to take on danger, difficulty, and opposition and move toward them with determination. Courage does not mean the absence of fear, but the willingness to move forward in spite of it.

Some stick their heads in the ground like an ostrich and hope the challenge will just go away. But that doesn't do much good, does it? It takes courage to face the challenges of life head-on. It takes courage to not give up, and that kind of courage starts with us being honest with ourselves.

Being Honest with Ourselves in a Positive Way

In order to live our best lives, we must be honest with ourselves. And that is hard! I have constantly confronted my own issues and shortcomings and have had to muster up the courage to be honest with myself. I realized that the only way I could grow my future and my finances was to get better. The only way I could get better was to be honest with myself and work on my shortcomings!

As I went through the challenges of life and experienced one setback after another, I was jolted into the reality that to have a better life, I needed to make a commitment to get better. That didn't mean that I didn't love myself or feel good about myself; it meant I loved myself enough to *work* on myself. I love the quote "What is your biggest room?" The answer should always be "Your room for improvement!" It never stops and never ends!

Part of the challenge I see in people who I coach is the bad habit of asking themselves questions that are dead-end, no-win questions. They tell me they wake up in the morning and place their head in their hands and ask, "What am I doing with my life?" And the answers they get are consistently negative. The answers would be "You are wasting your life!" or "You are going nowhere and doing nothing!" or "Your life is a hot mess!" One bad answer after another. The problem is, because they are asking such dead-end, no-win questions, they are only going to get dead-end, no-win answers.

I tell them how critically important it is to have different questions. How critical it is to change their questions from dead-end, no-win questions to positive, possibility-focused questions. Rather than asking, "What am I doing with my life?" I recommend they try a different approach. They should ask, "What can I do with my life?"

Each time I share this, people they say that everything changes! By asking themselves positive questions, they are able to get positive answers. When they asked questions about the future, about what they could do with their lives, their answers were better; they would say, "I can change it" or "I can turn it around" or "I can be excellent and create a reputation for excellence that will positively enhance my impact and my income!"

People told me they changed when they were willing to be honest with themselves and face their own issues honestly. Just as an alcoholic doesn't get better until they realize that a real problem exists, we, too, only get better when we realize that we need to change. The worst lies we ever tell are the lies we tell ourselves.

One of the biggest challenges to success is the challenge to overcome the enemy within—the enemy we see in the mirror every day. Just like the Michael Jackson song "Man in the Mirror" says, we have to start with the person we see reflected in the mirror each day. If we are going to be the best we can be, we must start with ourselves. We must be willing to change our ways and make a commitment to get better and to grow—personally and professionally. And in order to change, we must have the courage to be honest with ourselves. We must be willing to confront our self-limiting beliefs and the behaviors that keep us from living our best lives.

I interviewed Chris Gardner on my Sirius XM show, and he is the real Pursuit of Happyness guy that mega movie star Will Smith portrayed in the movie, *The Pursuit of Happyness*. Chris Gardner was a single dad who ended up homeless and yet changed his life and became a very successful stockbroker. In the interview Chris said, "Please remember that wherever you are in life, you drove there! Yet, also remember, that wherever you are, you can drive out!" There is one other quote from that movie that I really love: "The world is your oyster, yet it is up to you to go out and find the pearls!" I encourage you to make up your mind to drive out of whatever situation you find yourself in, and take the action to find the pearls in your world!

The Importance of Lifelong Learning

If you're going to be all that you can be and have the potential to be, then you must make a commitment to lifelong learning. This means you have made the commitment to continue to read and grow yourself in order to grow your future. You can never stop learning. For those who are serious about success, school never ends.

I had been talking to audiences about the importance of lifelong learning and as I preached it to them, I was also preaching it to myself. Yet, I was not completely doing what I was preaching. I was reading a book a week and listening to audios in the car and working on myself, but I still had something I had been talking about for years but had not done. For years I had been talking about going back to school and getting my doctorate, but I kept saying to myself that I was too busy. I had been saying that to myself for a long time—for years.

After I got married, we started a family, then I started my speaking and publishing business, and then I started hosting my radio and television programs. And all this time I kept saying I wasn't able to stop and go back to school. Or maybe in reality I didn't want to take the time to stop and go back to school.

Yet the opportunity came to me where I had to finally put up or shut up.

I was speaking at the Crystal Cathedral in Garden Grove, California, for the international broadcast of *The Hour of Power* television show. In the congregation that morning was the president of the California Graduate School of Theology. He came up to me after the service and said he wanted me to be the graduation speaker for their next graduation. He said it was a year off, but they really liked to get inspirational people on the calendar in advance. He said my message would be perfect for his students and he would call me in a couple of days to work out the details. By the time he called me he said he had done some research online and realized that my speaking fee was way outside of their budget. So he asked me if I would be willing to take a small honorarium and an honorary doctoral degree. I realized this was a moment where I had to put up or shut up, so I offered him a counteroffer. I proposed that I speak for free, and in exchange for the graduation speech, that I be allowed to work for my doctorate. He was puzzled and said, "Why would you want to work for your doctorate when you can get an honorary doctorate?" I shared with him that I had learned something over my many years of speaking, and my many years of interviewing great achievers on my Sirius XM show. I had learned that it is not just hitting the goal that makes you great, but what you become in the process of pushing and prodding to achieve that goal that really ultimately grows you into a person of greatness.

Dr. Willie Jolley at his graduation from the California Graduate School of Theology with former Chancellor Dr. Paul H. Lee.

He said he loved that concept. He told me he would take it back to the school's board of trustees and would get back to me. He called me the next day and said we had a deal.

So for the next year I shuttled back and forth to California and wrote four major papers and a 150-page dissertation. Let me tell you, it was hard! Plus, it was humbling! I was humbled when I wrote my first paper. I wrote the paper a couple days before it was due and thought it was a great paper, with my best stuff.

I submitted it and looked forward to a great grade. I came in for the class and the professor told me how much he loved my books; he had read all of them. Then he handed me my paper and it had a Big Fat "F" on it! He told me that I got the "F" because I wrote about what I already knew. He said, "Willie, school is not for what you already know, but for learning and engaging our minds with new information. You need to go to the library and do research." Ouch!

It was humbling, but he was right. So I decided to shut down my business and started going to the library every day from 9 to 5. It was quite an experience for a fifty-plus-year-old man to sit in a library every day with people in their twenties and thirties. Yet I did it! And a year later on the third Saturday in May, I graduated from the California Graduate School of Theology with a doctorate in faith-driven achievement!

I am encouraging you to not let your age or your stage in life stop you from continuing to develop yourself and develop your future. Take some classes, go back to school, and continue to pursue your personal excellence. That is part of how you develop the leader within. That is part of how you stand up to be counted.

Hurts, Habits, Hang-ups

Our hurts, habits, and hang-ups hold us back.

Hurts

There is a story of a little boy who smelled the hot cherry pie his mother had made and put on top of the stove to cool. This little boy wanted to sneak a piece of the pie, so he grabbed the pan—and burned his hand! He burned his hand and never forgot the hurt, so he never touched another cherry pie, hot or cold. He missed out on good cherry pie because of a past hurt.

In life, we can miss out on a lot more than cherry pie. Past hurts can fill us with fear and keep us from even giving our dreams a chance. Past hurts can make us give up without even trying. Many people have great talents and abilities but do nothing with them because someone in their past has hurt them with negative words or actions. Sometimes the hurts come from people you love and trust; their negative thinking can alter your life forever.

One time I gave a speech in Columbus, Ohio, at the Hyatt Hotel. A few hours before the program began, I went to get a sound check, and met the gentleman preparing to sing the national anthem. He started to warm up and sing a few scales, and I realized that he had a beautiful voice. I knew I was going to get a blessing by hearing him sing that evening. Yet as he started to rehearse, a woman who was mopping the floor hollered to another woman, "Hey, Marge, did you get the name of the cat that died?" and she started laughing.

I looked at that woman in total amazement and said, "How can you be so negative?" Fortunately, the singer did not hear her comment! She said, "Oh, I was just playing." Even though she thought it was harmless fun, it was not. Sticks and stones can break our bones, and words can hurt us. In fact, words can break our spirits and kill our initiative to try! What that woman said is the same kind of jokes that negative parents say to their children. Unfortunately, such jokes have a lifelong impact on the self-esteem and, eventually, the achievement of their children. Just think: If Nat King Cole, Whitney Houston, Celine Deon, Aretha Franklin, Michael Jackson, Barbra Streisand, Luciano Pavarotti, or Marian Anderson had been given negative feedback from someone who was "just having some fun," that might have influenced them to never sing again. Not only would their lives have been drastically different, but so would ours—and we would be poorer because of it.

Be careful of your words, both to others and to yourself. If you hear them enough you, too, can stumble through life thinking you were born to lose, when in reality you were born to win.

I especially encourage you to never, ever speak in negative terms to your children. You might think it has no impact, but often children take everything their parents say as gospel, even if it is only a joke. When my children were little someone told me this concept. They recommended that I tell my children that they have greatness in them and to say it every day. So I started doing it. Initially my kids thought it sounded crazy as I said, "Good morning! By the way, you have greatness in you! Have a great day!" And then I would walk off. No big thing, just a way to affirm daily that they were destined for great things. I kept doing it every day. Months went by, and one day I got a call from my son's school. There had been an incident. My son was playing ball with another friend and a little boy came and took the ball. My son took the ball back and the little boy, who was smaller than my son, slapped my son. My son balled up his fist and then said, "Nope, you can't make me go there!" The teacher who witnessed it told the principal. They were calling me to let me know that he would be given a special leadership award at an upcoming assembly and hoped we could attend! Wow, was I relieved! If you want great kids, speak greatness into them at every opportunity you can. I can tell you it works.

Habits

We have habits that we know are bad for us, yet we continue to repeat them because we are not willing to change. We are not willing to go through the struggle and discipline of change. We are not willing to face the habits and confront the pain that it will take to change! One example from my life is the bad habit I had for many years of being late. I would always put too much on my schedule, and as a result, I would end up cutting it much too close or being late. One day, I arrived late for a scheduled radio session. The engineer told me he had canceled a paid date to get me in and that my lateness had cost him a very important client! I was so embarrassed and pained by the expression on his face that I realized I had to change that habit—and I did!

Do you have some bad habits that are impacting your life? Are there some habits that are hurting you or hurting others you care about? If so, change them! Famed dictionary writer Dr. Samuel Johnson wrote, "The diminutive chains of habit are seldom heavy enough to be felt, until they are too strong to be broken!"

Hang-ups

Finally, we have hang-ups that continually put us in bad situations and pull us down and pull us back. Hang-ups are the issues that we have that negatively impact our efforts and actions. The hang-ups act like an invisible elastic band around our waists that pull us back every time we take a few steps forward. Every time we try to get going and get moving, the hang-ups appear. Like a rubber band, they snap us back to our original positions. We are moving and active, but we are not getting anywhere. To succeed we must have the courage to face the enemies within, to face our hang-ups and change them so we can stop sabotaging our own success. We must be honest with ourselves and make the decision to address these hang-ups, so we can make the changes to get better. Only then can we do more, be more, and achieve more!

In my book *A Setback Is a Setup for a Comeback,* I share the formula for overcoming hang-ups and other self-limiting and self-destructive issues. In the book, I share that we must Face It, Trace It, Erase It, and Replace It. First, we must Face It. We must face the issue and be honest with ourselves that we have an issue. Whether it is a drug issue, alcohol issue, sex issue, anger issue, or a low self-esteem issue, we must start by facing it. After acknowledging there is a problem, the next thing I do is pray. I told you earlier, when I have a setback I always take time to pray for wisdom and courage. I pray for wisdom so I can know what to do; and courage so I will be strong enough to do what is necessary. I do not always pray for God to fix it. Rather, I pray for God to help me face it, because I know if I can face it, then He can help me fix it! After I pray, then I know it is time to act, because prayer and action go hand in hand. First pray, then PUSH, which stands for Push (Take Action) Until Something Happens. You must take action. James 2:20 (NKJV) says: "Faith without works is dead." Faith must be manifested in action. Second, we need to Trace It, which means to see where it started in our lives or where we made the error in judgment that created the issue. You must find where the issue springs from. What is the source of this issue that continues to hang you up? Successful people learn from past mistakes and make adjustments for the future. If you don't learn from the past, you can create a cycle of mistakes, which leads to you beating yourself up. This leads to lower self-esteem, which leads to negative feelings about yourself and your decisions, which leads to more bad decisions. Then you start the cycle over again with more negative self-talk and lower esteem and more bad decisions. *Stop the Madness!* If you make a mistake, so be it. Learn from it and keep going.

Next you must Erase It! Get the mistake out of your system and out of your life. We all make mistakes, but only the unsuccessful dwell on them. The successful learn from them and move on. I have found that there are two types of mistakes: those that teach and those that destroy. We can either see those mistakes as learning experiences, or we can see them as death blows. We can see them either as our teacher or our undertaker. It is your choice: I recommend that you make them your teacher.

Once you have faced it, traced it, and erased it, then you must replace it. There might be hang-ups, issues, and items in your life that just beg to be replaced. Do them a favor and grant them their wish; leave them alone and replace them. Replace the negative element with a positive element and move to a place of peace, purpose, and passion. Stop letting the hang-ups hang you up and hang you out to dry. No! Hang up on your hang-ups. Let them go.

The Impact of a Bounce-Back Attitude

I love to share the story of how as children my brother and I would wrestle and tussle with each other so much that our parents decided to get one of those punching bags with the weighted base and the big smiling face. When you hit the bag, it would go down temporarily but quickly bounce back up. We would hit that bag every day, trying to keep it down, but it would always bounce back up, with that big smiling face. We did everything we could to try to knock the bag down and keep it down, but it would keep bouncing back up. We eventually got bored with the bag and left it alone and went looking for other trouble to get into (and my parents would typically reward our efforts with a spanking). Yet every now and then, we would revisit the bag. We would sneak up from behind and in unison we would hit it with everything we had. But it would always bounce back up. And it always had that same big smiling face!

There is a life lesson in this. Life will hit you and occasionally knock you down. But you must bounce back up, and keep bouncing back up. And always keep that big smile on your face! Eventually, life will get bored with you and go find a wimp it can keep down. But then, when you least need it or expect it, life will sneak up on your blind side and hit you with everything it has. That is when it is necessary to go deep within and pull up all the strength you have and look life in the eye and say, "You can knock me down, but you will never keep me down, because I am a comeback kid!"

Every now and then, if you are willing to stand up to life and keep fighting for your dream, life will recognize that you are absolutely serious about your success and will leave you alone to find a wimp who will quickly give up and give in. Again, keep fighting for your dreams. It might not happen as quickly as you like, but to those who persist, amazing results can come your way!

Scripture tells of a person who comes to a neighbor's house around midnight and knocks on the door to ask for some bread for friends who have come to visit. The neighbor had gone to bed, but reluctantly comes to the window and says that he and his family have gone to bed for the night and the person should come back in the morning. The person keeps knocking and knocking and knocking. Eventually the neighbor comes to the door and gives the person the bread. The Bible states that the neighbor gave the person bread not because of their friendship but rather because of importunity, which means unrelenting persistence. You must persist if you are going to win in life and in business!

Success does not always come when you want it, and therefore you must persist. Case in point: A few years ago I was inducted into the National Speakers Association Speaker Hall of Fame, after many years of being rejected. It was quite an honor and joy to finally win the award. Yet, the biggest award was the lesson that I learned, which was how to use rejection as motivation to keep working on myself and to make the commitment to continue to get better.

During my early years in the speaking business, I was honored to be tabbed by Les Brown to join the Music and Motivation Tour, and after a year on the tour Les Brown nominated me for the Speaker Hall of Fame. I did not win. I was nominated the next year by another Hall of Fame recipient, and again did not get selected. I got nominated the next year and the next—but I did not win! I had to fight discouragement.

Discouragement, by definition, is when we lose heart and lose our courage to keep trying. I am encouraging you to not let discouragement take away your courage to keep fighting. We all get disappointed, but we do not have to let discouragement steal our courage. Rather than letting it take your courage, I recommend you keep getting better. Each failure forced me to continue to get better and learn to stay positive in the process. To get bitter or to get better were my only options. When we have a problem, it is not so much the problem we face, but the decision we must make. Do we get bitter or get *better*?

It became my goal to make a commitment to work on myself and to do whatever was necessary to grow into the type of person who was worthy of such an honor. Getting up earlier. Staying up later. Reading more. Studying more. Practicing more. Each time I did not get the award, I worked even harder on myself.

Finally, after years and years of hard work, being nominated twelve times, I was inducted into the Speaker Hall of Fame. The lesson I learned was that the real gift was in going through the process of growing myself. The real honor came in the lessons I learned along the way.

Murphy's Law

As you start out after your goals and dreams, watch out for Murphy (anything that can go wrong will go wrong). Time and time again, Murphy will come and visit you. Murphy's Law says that stuff will happen to discourage you and throw you off course at the worst possible moment. You will have challenges and setbacks. The actor Marlon Brando once said, "The Messenger of Misery (Murphy) comes to visit everyone!" Murphy has your name, address, and telephone number on a piece of paper and is coming to visit you sooner or later. A gentleman came up to me after a program and said that Murphy didn't come to visit him, Murphy had a room at his house! I literally laughed out loud.

Yet, sometimes the situation is beyond something you can laugh at, but can knock you down and out. It might be a tough situation that will test you to the core. My chapter in *Chicken Soup for the Soul—Stories of Faith: Inspirational Stories of Hope, Devotion, Faith, and Miracles* is a story that documents my experiences of losing my mother, my brother (who was my only sibling), and my father-in-law (who was my mentor and surrogate father) in the span of twenty-five days. It was a devastating period. This was a time when I had to rely on my faith and my attitude to keep me from losing my mind. As a result of that experience I learned that I had to decide whether I would curse because a rose bush had thorns or celebrate because the thorn bush had roses. In other words, I had to decide whether I would curse because they were gone or celebrate that they had come my way. I decided to celebrate! I encourage you to do the same when you lose someone you love. Make the decision to reframe the loss from one of cursing a rose bush having thorns to celebrating because a thorn bush has roses.

That decision helped me to reframe my thinking and changed my attitude, which allowed me to get out of my pit of depression and get to a place of gratitude for the fact that my loved ones came my way. I encourage you to use this question when you are grieving the loss of someone dear to you, and you, too, will see how you will be lifted. Choose to have a positive attitude, even in the midst of negative, difficult times. I can attest it is not only possible, but also very doable.

I followed the three basic guidelines to get through the tough times:

1. Seek help from your family, your friends, and your faith. Also, get grief counseling. See counseling as an asset, not a liability. If you broke your arm, what would you do? You would go to the doctor! Yet many people have broken hearts and refuse to go get

professional help. They try to heal it themselves. Counseling does not make you weak; it helps to keep you strong.

2. Talk to yourself and say, "Life does not have to be perfect to be wonderful!" Ask yourself that question I asked myself in my loss: Do I curse because a rose bush has thorns, or do I celebrate because a thorn bush has roses? Do I curse because the person or situation is no longer the same? Or do I celebrate because that person or that situation came my way?

3. Decide to have a positive attitude. Abraham Lincoln said, "Most people are about as happy as they choose to be." Choose to be happy. Choose an attitude of gratitude.

Step Up!

Step Up to the Plate and Swing for the Fences

The fourth step to personal five-star success is to step up. You must step up to the plate in life and give it your best shot!

To have great success, you must consistently swing for the fences. In my upcoming book, *Stop Playing Small: If You Want to Win Big You Must Play Big!*, seven steps are outlined for big success:

1. Stop playing small. Start small but always think big and play bigger than you think you can!
2. Stop making excuses. Start taking action.
3. Stop whining. Start winning.
4. Stop worrying. Start using your faith to succeed.
5. Stop waiting. Start making your dreams happen now.
6. Stop waiting for God to drop stuff in your lap. Start putting your lap where God is dropping stuff.

7. Stop just talking about what you want to do. Start doing what you want to do, *then* talk about it!

Mark Sanborn, the author of the best-selling book *The Fred Factor*, says, "One of the keys to greater personal and professional success is to remember the 'ABCD principle,' which means to always stay focused on going 'Above and Beyond the Call of Duty!' In terms of job descriptions, some say, 'That is not my job!' But winners say, 'It's all my job! Whatever needs to be done to get the job done is my job!'"

Be Willing to Fail

Every day, you must step up and give your best shot, with the understanding that sometimes you will fail. But fail or not, you must keep swinging for the fences. Life, like baseball, is a game of risk and reward. A batter stands at the plate facing a pitcher. The pitcher's job is to throw the ball with such velocity that the batter is unable to hit it. The batter stands at the plate with a wooden bat. The risk comes in how much effort the batter is willing to expend in trying to hit the ball. Does he play it safe and just try to bunt (tap the ball), which is an easy option? Or does he focus and go all in and try to hit the ball out the park, which increases the risk that he might strike out? Sometimes they miss, but when they hit the ball with all their might, they knock it out of the park. The great ones make their name by swinging for the fences. I recommend that you get a "swing for the fences" mindset and keep giving it your all, in whatever you want to succeed at in life.

Sometimes the pitcher throws a curve ball. This ball is a pitch that looks like it is perfect to hit, yet at the last moment it takes a strange twist, a curve. Life may throw you some curve balls too, disruptions that try to stall your progress. You will experience a setback, a twist of fate that will throw you off-track and distract you from your goal. But don't let the curve balls stop you; just learn the strategies for turning the curve ball into a grand slam home run!

In interviews, baseball players say that the way to hit a curve is to keep your eye on the ball, step up, step in, and give it your best shot. Give it your all! I recommend the same strategy in succeeding against life's curve balls. Keep your eye on the goal. Step up to the challenge. Step in and give it your best shot!

Statistics show that the great home-run hitters in baseball usually strike out more than they succeed; yet they keep swinging for the fences. Hank Aaron had twice as many strikeouts as he had home runs. But every time he stepped to the plate he gave it his all. Sometimes he missed, but when he hit it, he knocked it out of the park! When you get your chance to do what you do, make a commitment to give it your best shot. Sometimes you will miss; but when you hit it, you will knock it out of the park!

Winners are willing to fail in order to succeed. Many people simply do not win because their fear of failure is stronger than their desire for success. People will not bring new ideas to the table because they are afraid of being humiliated if the ideas fail. Or they stay with the old way that has had only moderate success, rather than trying something new that could bring massive success. I know it can be frightening, but I encourage you to face your fears and pursue your dreams.

Failure is painful, but not final—unless you choose for it to be final. On the other hand, nothing is more painful than regret, to look back over your life and wonder what could have been if you had just had the courage to give it a shot!

There is a story about the man on his deathbed, surrounded by ghoulish creatures with bulging eyes and hideous voices. They spoke to him with anger, saying, "We are the dreams that were given to you to bring to life, yet because of your fear and lack of faith you never gave us a chance. So we must now die with you! How dare you!"

Have courage and swing for the fences. You might miss, but failure is not final; regret can be! Pursue excellence and continue to be willing to fail in order to succeed and keep growing your success and your reputation in the marketplace.

Don't Quit

Quitters never win, and winners never quit. A simple phrase that has been around for centuries, yet a phrase that people have needed to be reminded of daily! It's as simple as that: You must not quit! We must learn strategies for handling the changes and challenges of life. Tough times do not last, but tough people do. You must not just *go* through these tough times; you must *grow* through tough times. I recommend you stay positive, even in tough moments, and never give up.

A few years ago I tore ligaments in my foot while playing tennis and it was a challenging situation but also a great opportunity to learn and grow. As I reflected on the situation, I realized that some of our greatest setbacks are also some of the best training grounds for creating a winner's mindset. I went to the podiatrist and she said that my injury was severe, just a millimeter from needing major foot surgery. She put a soft cast and walking boot on my foot and said she figured I would take about eight weeks to heal. I told her I didn't have eight weeks because I had a tennis tournament in five weeks. I told her I planned to be completely healed in five weeks and planned to play in the tournament. She looked at me and said, "Anyone else I would say they are crazy, but you and your positive thinking can be hard to gauge!" She said I needed to come back in four weeks and she would check my progress and let me know how I was doing.

I went home and started reading everything I could about positive healing and started speaking about my foot being completely healed in record time. I continued to work out every day, even with the boot on. A friend at the gym was a professor of psychology and neurology and he shared with me a healing process called psychoneuro immunology. He shared how positive thinking and positive conversation can have a profound impact on healing. He recommended I not only think and speak in positive terms but also actually talk to my body and my foot and continue to tell it that it is healed. Once I got that much investment in my healing I added one more element. I prayed and asked all my friends to pray, because I believe in the power of prayer.

Every day I went through the process and every day I felt stronger. And in four weeks I went back for my checkup. My podiatrist said, "I am amazed! Your X-ray shows a completely healed foot!" I thanked her, gave her back the boot, and walked out and went to the tennis court and played a couple of sets of tennis. The lesson I learned was that positive thinking, positive speaking, and prayer are a powerful combination to help you reach your goals. Stay positive and never quit speaking and acting in a positive manner!

Keep Your Eye on the Prize

What do you do when you have started out on your goals and dreams, and then calamity strikes? I say first, you must decide to keep your eyes on the prize and not on the problems. Indeed, it is through the problems and pain of life that we grow; that is why we call them "growing pains." Yet, we must decide whether we will *go* through the problems or *grow* through the problems. That decision will determine our actions, and our actions will determine our results.

Sometimes life will knock you down and try to knock you out. Yet, I encourage you to pick yourself up, dust yourself off, catch your breath, and get moving again in the direction of your goals.

Some time ago I heard the story of a marathon runner who went to war and was involved in a mortar accident and lost his legs. He lost so much of his lower body that a prosthesis was not possible. He was down, but he made up his mind that he was not out. When he recovered from his injuries, he told the doctors that the first thing he wanted to do was to start training for another marathon. They reminded him that he had no legs and that it would be almost impossible to move around without a wheelchair. Any movement he made beyond his wheelchair would require him swinging his body from spot to spot on his hands.

He thanked the doctors for their concern, but he had made up his mind that he was going to run another marathon without a wheelchair!

He started working on his goal, and worked for months on just swinging his body from spot to spot and moving around his house. Then he started working on going farther. He trained for almost a year and was finally able to swing himself a mile! He kept on training and got up to two miles, then three miles, and then four miles and continued to train until he felt he was ready to try twenty-six miles. He started the race with all the other able-bodied racers. The able-bodied runners all finished that same day, some in a few hours, but not him. It took him two days of nonstop swinging his body from one spot to another.

When he finally crossed the finish line, the only people there were his family and a single newspaper reporter. As he crossed the finish line, with his hands bloodied and his stumps raw, the reporter could not believe he had continued, considering the intense pain he must have been experiencing. As his family members prepared to take him to the hospital, the reporter asked how it was that the pain did not stop him. He replied, "Yes, it was painful, but every time the pain became intense, I would focus my energy on the goal, and I would think about how I would feel crossing the finish line! The joy I would get from achieving the prize was more powerful than the pain of the problem."

I want you to know you will have some challenges in your quest for success, but please do not stop. Do not give up. Do not let it derail your success. Focus on the prize of achieving your goal rather than the pain of the problem. If you do, you will see that in time your prizes will grow and your problems will shrink, and most of all, you will *grow yourself and grow your success*! Through my physical challenge I learned firsthand that my friend W. Mitchell, the award-winning inspirational speaker who survived two life-altering accidents and refused to give up on his dreams, is absolutely right. W. Mitchell has become known as the man who was burned in a motorcycle crash and then paralyzed in an airplane accident, yet continues to share with people around the world that it doesn't matter what happens to you, because it's what you do about it that counts. I truly believe that a setback is nothing but a setup for a comeback, and I am a comeback kid. How about you?

Stretch Yourself

I love this quote by Jim Rohn, author and personal development expert: "Don't wish that the problem were smaller, wish that you were bigger!" I believe that we can grow and stretch beyond what we think we can do and literally do much more. I believe that the best way to predict the future is to create the future, and so get up, get dreaming, get going, get stretching, and get to really living life at another level.

Use the changes and challenges of life to propel yourself to that next level. I recommend that we use the three C's for Success: change, challenge, and choices as the guide.

Change

Someone once said that the only constant in life is change, which is a part of the success process, but it takes work to get through the process.

Change is constant and uncomfortable. We do not want to change! No matter how many books we read or seminars we attend in regard to "embracing change," it is still uncomfortable. It is uncomfortable because we are creatures of habit and we tend to do what we have always done. Yet we must change if we want to grow.

Change by its very nature is uncomfortable. Try this exercise: Stop. Cross your arms, and look at which arm is on top. (I mean put the book down for a minute and cross those arms!) Now that you have found which one is on top, do it again and this time switch the arms. Did you notice how uncomfortable it is? The reason it is so uncomfortable is that you have been crossing your arms the same way since before you were born! Babies start crossing their arms in their mother's womb, and they never, ever change. We are creatures of habit and therefore it is very uncomfortable indeed to change. Yet change is necessary for growth, so we have to work on the habits that keep us from growing and succeeding at the highest levels.

As a full-time nightclub singer, I sang the song called "Everything Must Change!" I sang the song just about every night, but I really never noticed how profound the words were. Years later, I realized I'd been singing about a great truth. The lyrics say, *everything must change . . . nothing stays the same!* In fact, everything must change and only those who are quickest to embrace and adapt to change win at the highest levels!

All progress is the result of change. Everything you are experiencing at this moment is the result of change. This book is the result of change. If you are sitting in a room with light bulbs rather than candles, that is the result of change. If you are reading this book on a computer as an e-book, then that is a result of change. If you are listening to the audio version of this book or listening to a podcast or CD or seeing my message online or on a video or DVD, then that is the result of change. There was a time when there were no computers, no podcasts, no internet, no CDs, and no DVDs or videos! All of this progress is the result of *change*. So we should see change not as an enemy but as an ally. In doing so, we can live a better life.

If you have children, you remember when they were babies how they would move about by crawling. And one day, miraculously, they stood on their own two feet for the very first time. They weebled and wobbled and typically they fell down. But no parent ever said, "Stay down, baby!" Instead they said, "Get up! Try again! Come to Mommy! Come to Daddy! Try again!" The baby usually tries again and falls down again, but they keep trying and trying until they learn to stay up. They take the first step, then the second step, and then the third. When the baby falls down, sometimes they fall on their backside, but sometimes they fall on their face! But the parent doesn't stop them from falling and trying. They encourage them to try again, and again, and again.

Parents know that if babies do not fall and get back up, they will never learn to walk. And if babies do not fall and get back up, they will never learn to run, and never learn to maximize their ability. Yet many people who fail in their attempts to achieve a goal get discouraged and give up. In doing so, they short-circuit their long-term success and long-term possibilities.

See change as a struggle that is worth the effort.

Challenge

Whenever we have to go through change, we will automatically have a challenge. A challenge is whenever events of any kind push you from your place of normalcy and comfort. Challenges test your resolve and determination—obstacles, difficulties, and sometimes serious setbacks.

Yet, the setback does not have to be the end of the road; it can be a bend in the road. And when it is a bend in the road, you can change and go in another direction. In fact, the only ones who crash and burn are those who fail to change. (Like Wile E. Coyote in the *Road Runner* cartoon series who would not change his path and inevitably would run into the side of the mountain!) We must learn to navigate the winds of change and go with the changes in the road as we move along in life.

Friends, you will have some challenges in your quest for greater success, but please do not stop, do not give up, and do not let it derail your success. Focus on the prize of achieving your goal rather than the pain of the problem. If you do, you will see that in time your prizes will grow, and your problems will shrink, and most of all, you will *grow yourself and grow your success!*

Choices

Finally, after change and challenge we come face to face with the last C, which is choices. Success in life ultimately comes down to your choices. My friend Marlon Smith, the high-tech motivator and president of Success By Choice, is known for telling audiences that your "success is your choice." Success truly is a choice and not a chance. You must choose to succeed. You choose to sleep in or choose to get up and get busy. You choose to think big or you choose to think small. You choose to be positive or you choose to be negative. You choose to keep fighting for your dreams or you choose to give up.

We all have experiences we cannot control, and then we must make choices. We cannot choose what life throws at us, but we can choose how we respond to what life throws at us. We cannot control what happens to us or what happens around us, but we have complete control over what happens in us! Choose to have a positive outlook, a positive "up-look," and a positive "in-look."

Step It Up to the Next Level

After you step up to the plate and give it your best shot, you must step it up, which means to step up your game and play at another level. Find a way to consistently and continually better your best. The Japanese call it the "Kaizen" principle, which means finding a way to constantly better your best. When I go out to speak, I have a goal that my speech today will be better than yesterday's speech, yet I want tomorrow's speech to be better than today's. Because after today's speech I am going to go and work on my message and improve it—because I have a great desire to get better!

I have been named "One of the Outstanding Five Speakers in the World" by Toastmasters International, inducted into the Speaker Hall of Fame, and named A Legend of the Speaking Industry, yet I still feel I am just getting started. I realized that the key to getting this far was to keep trying to get better. I learned I cannot forget the bridge that brought me across—the bridge called "Better" that changed my business. It was making the commitment to get better and to look for ways to create constant and never-ending improvement that helped me grow as a speaker and as a person. It was the lessons learned about making a commitment to a never-ending pursuit of excellence that helped me grow.

Make a commitment to personal development. As long as you have life, keep working on getting better. Learn a new language or a new skill or take courses to take your present skills to another level. Not only does it make you better, but studies show that learning new languages and new skills strengthens your brain and helps to offset Alzheimer's disease. Whatever the reason you decide to make the commitment, I can tell you that when you change, things will change for you. Make a commitment to read one self-help, personal development book a month from here on out. There is a direct correlation between the books you read and the money you make. Readers are leaders, and those who read more books typically rise faster through the ranks.

Change, challenge, and choices are a part of the personal development program for winners. Stand up to life, stand up to yourself, and stand up to the changes and challenges of life and declare: "I am a winner and winners never quit and quitters never win! I am a winner!"

Think Up!

Make Up Your Mind to Win

The final step in your five-step process of personal transformation is to think up! Now, when I say "think up," I mean a few things. First, I literally mean I want you to think positive, upward thoughts, even in down times. This means you think about what positive things can happen, not what negative things might happen. In other words, to think up is *to think about your possibilities* and not get stuck thinking about the probabilities. Probability thinking would say that a former nightclub singer who got fired and was broke, busted, and discouraged would have very little chance to have a successful career as a professional speaker. Possibility thinking says, "Willie, give it a shot! You have always had a desire to inspire. Plus, you should never let your present circumstances determine your future possibilities. Go for it! Everything's possible!"

Second, to think up means to be a forward thinker, one who anticipates the needs of others and plans and prepares for the future. To be a forward thinker is to be like the ant, one of the most productive creatures on the face of the earth. Ants prepare for the winter while it is still summer. They do not let winter catch them without supplies to survive. They think winter all summer long.

To be a forward thinker is to have forethought about the goals that you are trying to reach. It also involves being proactive about what needs to be done rather than waiting for someone to tell you what to do. When hiring new staff, I always look for people who are forward thinkers; people who do not need to be told daily what they should do but rather think ahead and come up with ideas on how to reach our goals faster. Start planning and preparing and thinking about tomorrow *today*!

Third, to think up is to think beyond the ordinary and think extraordinary. There is a popular phrase that says "think outside the box." Nido Qubein, president of High Point University and business growth expert, says we should not only "think outside the box, but throw the box away!" If you are going to live a five-star existence and do what you enjoy doing, you must continue to pursue excellence, and often, you will have to think of new ways and try new tools to achieve your goals. For example, I was booked for two events on the same day, one in the morning in Maryland and another in the evening in Florida. Yet, due to a scheduling challenge with the president of the company, my presentation time had to be changed. They gave me a couple of days' notice, so we looked for ways to make it happen. We found that there were no flights available to get me from one event to the next in the appropriate time frame, and not even a private plane would work due to the distance and the short time between each event. We could not change the time for either event, so we had to think creatively. We had to "throw away the box." We had to think up!

I asked one of the clients if it would be okay for me to be there, yet not be there, physically. To be live, in real time, talking to them like I was physically there, but not really, physically there. He said, "Well, yeah. I guess so!" I suggested a "live" transmission to his group while I was in another city. He loved the idea! I found that Universal Studios had new equipment that was the next best thing to a hologram, where I could speak and answer questions, all in real time. I went to Orlando and spoke to my Maryland client from the Universal Studios. Then I rode to the other side of Orlando and spoke to the group. It was a smashing success and both clients were happy. Thinking up works!

A Man Who "Thought Up" Billions

A great example of someone who thinks up is Elon Musk, a man who some call today's Thomas Edison. He is a guy who is motivated, not primarily by making money, but rather by pursuing excellence. He learned early on that if you pursue excellence, and pursue it with a positive attitude, forward thinking, and the ability to think outside the box, you can change the world, and in the process, make a lot of money.

Elon Musk started as a small-time entrepreneur who was determined to push the envelope on technology and had a willingness to try new things and take old concepts and do them in a new way. He started a company with his brother called Zip2 to help people navigate big cities. The company struggled but eventually became successful and was bought by Compaq. When the company was sold, Elon became a multimillionaire, but he didn't see that as a stopping point. He was still anxious to pursue excellence. He used the money to help start another company to help people to move money in a new way. That company was Paypal. When Paypal was sold to eBay he netted more than $150 million.

After that, Musk could have retired and lived comfortably, yet he still had a desire to pursue excellence. He took his money from the Paypal sale and invested it in Space X, a company to develop space flight for consumers. The company struggled and he could have thrown in the towel and lived on his savings, but he maintained his positive attitude and his quest for excellence, and he rode out the storm. The company grew and after a number of failures in space flight, he succeeded in developing rockets that actually land themselves. What's more, while he was growing Space X he decided to disrupt the auto industry. So he cofounded a company called Tesla, which produces full-powered, long-distance, high-tech electric cars. Tesla went public and Musk became a billionaire, but again he continued to pursue excellence with a positive attitude!

His next venture was a solar energy company called Solar City, which also created more wealth. After that he created a company called Hyperloop, which creates high-speed travel, and another company called Boring, which looks to build high-speed, no-traffic underground highways. Musk has an unending quest for excellence. He continues to pursue new ideas and go after his goals with passion to show the world that an attitude of excellence can not only make a huge difference but also make a huge profit!

Make Up Your Mind to WIN!

How we think and what we think is very important. In his landmark book *Think and Grow Rich*, Napoleon Hill wrote, "Whatever the mind of man can conceive and believe it can achieve!" Earl Nightingale says that the reason most people don't succeed in life is not because of a lack of talent or ability, but because they simply don't think! The Bible says, "As a man thinketh, so as he is!" So, what are you thinking? In order to live a five-star life and have a five-star organization, we must make a commitment to think up, to think about the possibilities and create a plan to make your dreams come true.

One of the most effective techniques to get to the five-star lifestyle is to start with the end in mind. The end, the goal, is clearly placed in your mind, and then you start to think about how to most effectively reach that destination. Imagine starting on a long trip without taking time to map out your path. You get into your car and start driving without planning your route. That would be the makings of a disaster!

The next step is to make up your mind to do Whatever Is Necessary (WIN). You make up your mind that you are *committed* to winning in life and business. I believe there is nothing more powerful than a made-up mind! When you make up your mind that you are definitely going to achieve your goal and commit that you will not allow anything to stop you, you get amazing power. I mentioned earlier that the ant is one of God's most incredible creatures. The ant is a forward thinker and prepares for winter all summer, but that is not all that is amazing about the ant. The ant has a made-up mindset, a winner's mindset. Ants achieve their goal—or else. If you put a piece of bread in front of an ant and then place a row of bricks between the ant and the bread, the ant will do whatever is necessary to get to that bread. It will go around the bricks, or it will go over the bricks, or it will dig under the bricks, but rest assured it will get to the bread. The problem is that most people do not make up their minds in such a definitive manner. Most people say they want to achieve their goals, but very few are actually committed to achieving their goals. I say you should stretch and go big!

To get a winner's mindset you must be willing to keep going in spite of the obstacles. Make up your mind and commit to achieve your goals without any trepidation or hesitation. When you do this, you tend to win more of your goals. I encourage people to do what they were born to do or empowered to do. If you are a singer, then sing. If you are a dancer, then dance. If you are a runner, then you should run and if you are a leader who is also a winner, which everyone has the potential to be, then lead and make the decision to win! Winners win, not because they are destined to win but rather because they decide to win and then find a way to win. They are not sure how they are going to win; they just find a way to make it happen.

Joe Montana, the famous quarterback, developed his reputation as a player who seemed to always find a way to win. Michael Jordan, considered one of the greatest "winners" in the history of basketball, made a habit of finding a way to win.

Magic Johnson, the basketball-star-turned-entrepreneur, developed a winner's attitude as a youngster and it has helped him achieve amazing results. When he was in high school, he led his team to a state championship. When he was in college, he led his team to a national championship. When he entered the professional basketball ranks, he led his team to a world championship! When he was infected with HIV, many thought his days were numbered, but again, his winner's attitude helped him win against impossible odds. While fighting to build and protect his health, he entered the business ranks and won again. He has become one of America's most prolific entrepreneurs, with Magic Johnson theaters, restaurants, Starbucks coffee shops, and housing developments. Magic Johnson proves again that winners win. He has successfully lived with HIV for many years and continues to thrive.

Winners don't always know how they are going to win; they just expect to win and that creates a belief in their core that somehow they will win, and therefore they find a way to win over and over again! Even against impossible odds, they find a way to win.

Tossing Aside Self-Limitations

When we think of winning we usually think about those who are first or best in a contest, but that is not the totality of winning. Winning is also about overcoming our own self-limitations in order to reach a goal. Booker T. Washington said, "Greatness is not about what you achieve in life, but rather what you must overcome in order to achieve it!"

Winning is more than just crossing the finish line first. It is making a personal commitment to fight through the challenges in order achieve a goal. As we said earlier, winning by its pure definition is to "gain or get possession of a goal by exerting great effort." The person who runs a marathon without legs and finishes dead last is a winner once he or she crosses the finish line. Winning is not just about finishing first. It is also about gaining possession by exerting great effort! And most times, putting forth your greatest effort happens when we overcome our "self-limiting beliefs."

After being the first person to successfully climb Mount Everest, Sir Edmund Hillary said, "It is not the mountain we conquered, it is ourselves!" He said that in order to achieve his goal he had to overcome his doubts, fears, and the hesitancy and thoughts of quitting.

It takes great effort to win in life and the reason most people do not win is because they don't exert enough consistent effort. Many people start out with a sincere intention to achieve their goal, and they typically work hard for a while, but then the challenges come, and their efforts weaken. They don't sustain the effort and therefore don't accomplish the goal. What can change this occurrence? What can help people have greater success in their personal and professional endeavors? What can help people to sustain and maintain the momentum to actually have a string of winning moments? It is the development of a winner's attitude. It is a commitment to develop the will to win! Vince Lombardi put it like this: "The difference between a successful person and others is not a lack of strength or knowledge, but rather a lack of the will to win!"

As I have studied successful people over the years, I am always amazed at the similarities I have found in those who consistently win. What is most amazing is that these people are not really extraordinary personalities, but rather ordinary people who do extraordinary things. They are people who set out after a goal and refuse to give up until they achieve that goal. They are the people who make up their minds that they are not going to stop until they achieve the goal. I believe that is the key to their consistent success: They go forth with a made-up mind! That's right, the first key to developing the winner's edge is a made-up mind, which involves having a mindset where you are committed to achieve the goal.

How to Think Like a Winner

How do you get that winner's attitude? First, start by telling yourself you are a winner! Look in the mirror and tell yourself that you were born for greatness. It might sound strange, but I can attest that it works. Say it, then repeat that every time you look in the mirror at least three times a day. Next, make a habit of filling your mind up with the pure, the powerful, and the positive. How do you do this? Read one self-help book a month. Listen to twenty minutes of positive messages when you first wake up. Turn off the news for that first twenty minutes of your day. Refuse to participate in negative conversations. Find five small things daily that you are thankful for. Those actions will turn into a reservoir of possibilities! Then think about the great things that you want to achieve, and start preparing for them.

There is a story about a man who talked about owning a Bentley automobile he had seen at the auto show when the show came to his city. He hung pictures of the Bentley in his bedroom. He looked at the pictures every day. Then he lost his job and decided to start his own company. He started his company in his spare bedroom. One day he went into the garage and cleaned it out. When his family asked him why, he said, "Because that is where my Bentley is going to go!" They laughed and told him he had lost his mind, because he was barely making ends meet with his new company. But he didn't laugh; he just kept working on himself and his business, and preparing for the day he could park his Bentley in the garage.

He would go to the library every morning to read and study and work on his business plan and his success system. Then he would go to the garage every evening to work on cleaning the spot where his Bentley would go. Everyone continued to laugh at him and they thought he had lost his mind! He continued to work on himself and work on his dream—and about five years later he had built a successful business and was able to go to the dealership and get a Bentley. That day he drove his Bentley into the parking space he had been preparing in his garage!

On my desk, a sign reads, "Winners make things happen and losers let things happen!" Some people say it a little differently: "Some people make things happen, others watch what happened, and then the rest stand around and ask, 'What happened!'" Whatever way you want to say it, the truth remains that those who are winners are those who make a determined decision to win!

Obstacles to Our Own Success

When asked what keeps them from being a success, most people blame the government, or the economy, or their families, and some blame the "-isms" of life—you know, sexism, racism, ageism, and so forth. But the one thing that most people avoid putting on their blame list is the most important factor—themselves! We are the main obstacles to our success in life.

It has been said that success follows the 80/20 rule. In a corporate setting, the 80/20 dynamic says that 80 percent of the work usually comes from 20 percent of the people. In personal achievement, you can look at it this way: We are responsible for 80 percent of our failure to hit our goals and outside obstacles are only 20 percent of the problem. The old African proverb we quoted earlier is worth repeating: "If you can overcome the enemy on the inside, the enemy on the outside can do you no harm!" Or as Pogo said, "We have found the enemy and he is us!"

We must be brutally honest and come to the realization that we are the biggest challenge to our own success! If you want to win, you must stop letting things happen and start making things happen. Remember, when all is said and done, more is said than done and it is still up to you. I know I was able to go from broke and busted to speaking to people all over the globe because I decided to stop talking about it and start doing it. I also decided to work on me, because ultimately, I was the main thing stopping me from becoming all I could become!

Once I caught on to the concept of personal development and lifelong learning, everything changed. And when I changed, things started to change for me!

Decide to Win/Refuse to Lose!

During a twenty-three-hour flight to Japan, I had planned to finish writing the final few chapters for a new book that was due upon my return to America. After boarding the flight, I settled in my seat and was ready to get to work. I pressed the power button on the computer, eagerly waiting for the screen to light up—but nothing happened! The computer would not come on. I tried and tried and tried again, but nothing happened. I soon realized that the screen was broken and the computer was not going to work.

At this point, I was not only disappointed, but I was also really frustrated. But I remembered a quote I'd read years ago, "When things go wrong, and you are faced with great challenges, you don't have just a problem to deal with, you have a decision to make." So, I made the decision and moved on to Plan B. I used my cell phone to dictate and to type! The spelling was not perfect, the keyboard was small, and my fingers were cramped, but I got the job done!

Things will always attempt to distract and disrupt you from accomplishing your goals. When these challenges appear in your life, remember: It's not just a problem you need to deal with; it's a decision you have to make. Decide to win, refuse to lose, and move forward in spite of the challenges.

• • •

What challenges are stopping you? What issues have kept you from accomplishing your goals? And most importantly, what are you going to do about it? I encourage you to keep learning, keep striving, and never give up. Don't let the challenges keep you from reaching your goals. Decide to win, refuse to lose— and keep striving!

It starts with a winner's attitude, which includes a made-up mind that says, "I am going to win!" It also includes an expectation that this is going to happen somehow, some way. I encourage you to make up your mind to win. The question is, are you willing to stretch beyond your comfort zone?

Try this exercise. Stand up. Turn your body as far as you absolutely can to the right. (Do it now. I'll wait for you!) Now that you have gone as far as you absolutely can to the right, I want you to do it again and this time try to go even farther. (I'll wait again. For you, I would be willing to wait all day.) Did you notice how much farther you went when you pushed it? The same is true for your goals and dreams! That said, I have some important homework for you to do.

One of the ways to get your dreams and goals clear is to use this exercise. Imagine you went to the doctor today and he told you that you have a rare illness. This illness guarantees you will be dead a year from now—but it also guarantees that anything you attempt, anything you try, you will achieve! What ten things would you attempt if you knew you could not fail? Write those ten things down on a piece of paper. Think as big as you can and dream as big as you can. Go as far as you can, and once you get there you will see that you can go even farther! Make sure to do your homework. What do you have to fear, and what do you have to lose? Give it a shot!

The Power of Setting Goals

Do you want *massive success*? Do you want *huge results*? In my first book, *It Only Takes a Minute to Change Your Life*, I wrote about Arnold Schwarzenegger, who has been a world champion bodybuilder, a movie star, and the governor of California. Arnold discovered some of the secrets to massive success and you can use those same tips to help make your dreams come true!

Although Arnold Schwarzenegger left Austria with only a few possessions, he left with something more important than money and things—a dream and the determination to make that dream become reality. He wrote his dream down on an index card that he called his "personal contract," which was a contract he made with himself.

The card had some handwritten goals. Arnold read it daily and made a vow to himself that he would make those goals into realities. The goals were: (1) to become the greatest bodybuilder of all time, (2) to become a wealthy movie star, (3) to become successful in politics!

Arnold Schwarzenegger became one of the greatest bodybuilders of all time and the youngest Mr. Universe award winner ever. He also won the Mr. Olympia title seven times before retiring to begin a career making movies. Arnold Schwarzenegger's first movie featured him as a bodybuilder, but he continued to grow his acting skills. In time, he became one of the highest paid movie stars in the business.

Arnold Schwarzenegger's next goal was to become politically active, first by becoming the chair of the President's Committee on Physical Fitness and then becoming active in the National Republican Party. Yet he still knew there were bigger fish to fry and bigger achievements to accomplish. He reread his "personal contract" and realized that his goal was to become *successful* in politics. He set out to accomplish that goal, and he did it! He became governor of California.

In the process of achieving success in America, Arnold learned the power of goals and how clear goals and a commitment to those goals can transform your life, your finances, and your future. He learned how to make his goals into realities and developed the confidence necessary to make that happen. Arnold has shown that there is power in setting goals, and those who learn how to set clear goals and make a commitment to achieving those goals are the ones who will achieve incredible results!

Arnold Schwarzenegger gives us more than a clear example of the power of goals. He also provides a clear example of the mindset of winners. Winners win! They have a winner's mindset and a winner's attitude and they expect to win. From Arnold we learn the secrets to long-term success. First, have a vision. Second, set goals. Third, make a commitment to those goals. Then make a commitment to your commitments. And finally, never give up!

If you are willing to dream big and go out and do the necessary work to turn those goals into realities, then you too can do what others call impossible! Let us all learn from Arnold Schwarzenegger: There is power in setting goals. Scripture says, "Write the vision, and make it plain that he who reads it may run the race!" Write your goals and make them clear and focused. Then get busy going about the business of achieving those goals. If you do, then in time you can start to make history and do those things that others say are impossible—and in the process you can start to actually live your dreams!

Goals vs. Commitments

Dr. Dennis Kimbro, the international speaker, author, and success expert, says we should have goals, but we should also have commitments. The goals are items we *would like* to achieve, yet the commitments are the things that we *must* achieve! In an interview with Dennis on my XM radio show, he said, "Willie, you have been married for over thirty years. When you got married, did you set a goal to stay married or did you make the commitment? I believe that the reason you have been married for over thirty years is because you made a commitment to stay married, rather than setting a goal to stay married." And you know what? Dennis was right!

What are your goals and what are your commitments? Stop right now! Write a list of ten things you would like to achieve. Then write down ten things that you are *committed* to achieve!

Goals: What I *would like* to achieve!

1. _____
2. _____
3. _____
4. _____
5. _____
6. _____
7. _____
8. _____
9. _____
10. _____

Commitments: What I *must* achieve!

1. _____
2. _____
3. _____

4. _____

5. _____

6. _____

7. _____

8. _____

9. _____

10. _____

How Badly Do You Want to Achieve It? The Power of Desire!

I have focused a great deal over the years on the power and impact of desire and the value of asking oneself, "How badly do you want to achieve your goal?" Desire is a critical element in the quest for success. No matter what you attempt, you will always have obstacles and hurdles. It is your desire that ultimately keeps you on track to achieve your goals.

Imagine you come home after a long day of working hard and there is absolutely nothing in the house to eat. What are you going to do? Most people give me one of the following answers:

Go to the grocery store.

Go to a fast food restaurant.

Go to a convenience store.

Go to a friend's house.

Now imagine:

That the grocery store is closed.

The fast food restaurant had a power failure and has no food prepared.

The convenience store has not gotten their food shipment in today and there is no food at this time.

Your friend is not home.

What are you going to do? Go somewhere else, try another friend's home? Try another restaurant? If you notice, you did not say you would give up. Why? Because when you are really hungry, you don't even think about giving up!

A "soda at midnight" is an analogy I often share with audiences. You must have great desire and great determination to get a soda at midnight if that's what you want. Many people may say that "they want it really bad," but the definitive question is how bad is "really bad" to you?

Imagine one person wakes up at midnight and says, "I want a soda and I want it really bad!" That person gets up, walks to the refrigerator, but finds no sodas, walks to the window, opens the shades, and sees that it's snowing. The first person then checks the refrigerator one more time, still finds no sodas, and settles for a glass of water and goes back to bed, because they really did not want the soda *that bad*!

A second person wakes up around midnight and says, "I want a soda and I want it really bad!" That second person gets up, walks to the refrigerator, finds no sodas, walks to the window, opens the shades, and sees that it's snowing. The second person then checks the refrigerator one more time, still finds no sodas, and then puts on their coat and gloves and boots and walks to the corner store. But the corner store is closed, so the second person goes back home, settles for a glass of orange juice and goes back to bed. They really did not want the soda *that bad*!

A third person wakes up around midnight and says, "I want a soda and I want it really bad!" That third person gets up, walks to the refrigerator, finds no sodas, walks to the window, opens the shades, and sees that it's snowing. The third person then checks the refrigerator one more time, still finds no sodas, and then puts on their coat and gloves and boots and walks to the corner store, but it is closed! Then the third person walks another quarter mile to the all-night market, but due to the snowstorm, it too is closed. The third person walks another half a mile to a gas station with a soda machine, but it is sold out! Yet, that third person keeps walking and trying, and walking and trying, and walking and trying to get a soda! They want it really bad and they are willing to keep going until they achieve their goal!

I shared that analogy during a radio interview and the radio show host was quiet for a few seconds. Then he said, "Willie

Jolley, that is the most ridiculous thing I have ever heard! Who is going to go out in a blizzard for a soda? That is ridiculous!"

I responded, "You are absolutely right—it is ridiculous! See, I have found that only those who attempt the ridiculous are those who achieve the spectacular!"

Oprah Winfrey was told it was ridiculous for a woman who came from her humble beginnings to think she could ever be a major television personality. Yet, she attempted the ridiculous and achieved the spectacular! *The Oprah Winfrey Show* was the number-one talk show for twenty-five seasons. Bill Gates was a Harvard University dropout. When he said he wanted to see a day where there would be a computer, with his software, in every school and home, he was told it was ridiculous. Yet he was willing to attempt the ridiculous and achieve the spectacular. He made the computer fast and affordable for the average consumer, and he became one of the wealthiest men in the world.

Desire is about your willingness to keep going in spite of the odds. It is about your willingness to do what others consider ridiculous in order to achieve your goal. You must have a winning appetite. How bad do you want it? How bad do you want to achieve your goals?

You must think ridiculous, outrageous thoughts, and then muster the courage to go after those goals and dreams so you, too, can experience the five-star life.

Are You Serious?

I got a note from an old friend from the days when I was singing in nightclubs. He said he had read about my induction into
the Speakers Hall of Fame and had seen me on television, and
wanted to know what I did to change my life. I told him that
I decided to change and that I learned it is true that once you
change, everything changes for you! I told him I made a commitment to grow me and to expand my thinking. I started a
course of self-development and made a commitment to read
positive books, listen to motivational audios, and attend lots of
motivational seminars.

In short, I told him that I decided to *get serious* about my
success. I made up my mind that I was going to do whatever was
necessary for success. I remember one of my mentors telling me
once that most people are "seriously, not serious about success!"
He said they talk about it, and talk about it, and talk about it,
but never do anything about it.

So I made up my mind to get serious! I made a commitment to get up early and stay up late. I made a commitment to
read everything I could about self-development, so I turned off
the television and invested heavily in books and tapes. I made
the commitment to get on the phone and make more sales
calls. I would get on the phone early in the morning and would
continue until late into the evening, and when I got tired and
wanted to stop, I would always make one more call. I made a

commitment that on a daily basis I would do more than I was paid to do, and give more than I was expected to give, and go further than I was asked to go.

He then asked me what three things I do on a daily basis. I told him that I start each day the same way with prayer and meditation. I thank God for each new morning that I get out of bed and I proudly proclaim, "This is the day that the Lord has made and I am glad and rejoice in it!" I have an attitude of gratitude because I have another opportunity to go out and live my dream! Second, I ask myself, "Willie, what would you do today if you were serious?" As I ponder that question, I list all of the answers. Finally, I review the list and get busy on achieving those items!

I told my friend that this was not rocket science, but it did take a "PHD"—Persistence, Hunger, and Determination! Most of all it takes a commitment to grow ourselves so we can grow our futures. Then we must make a commitment to that commitment! In other words, we must get serious about success! My question to you today is, what would you do today if you were serious?

CONCLUSION: YOU ARE A WINNER
And I Believe in You!

I want to congratulate you for reading this book and for reading all the way to the end. You are one of the special people. Statistics show that most people never read another self-help book after their last year of formal education. Statistics also show that most of those who pick up a book never read it. They participate in "shelf-help" rather than "self-help." You not only obtained this book (whether you purchased it or your office purchased it for you), but you also didn't just put it on a shelf. You decided to read this book, and you read it to the very end. I want to congratulate you and let you know that you are one of the people who I am expecting to win and to win big. And most of all I want you to know that I truly believe this and I truly believe in you!

I will close with a story about how someone else's belief in you can have a powerful and profound impact on your success. Many years ago I was in Philadelphia, Pennsylvania, at the opening session of the National Speakers Association Convention. On the day of the opening session of this convention, I was sitting with friends in the far back corner of the ballroom. As I sat there laughing and joking with my friends, a photographer came over to me and asked me if I could walk with him to the other side of the ballroom so he could take a picture with me and a couple other speakers. I said, "Sure!"

As we walked across the board room, the photographer told me that he was very excited because the three speakers who had the greatest impact on his business were all in that room that evening. He said he couldn't believe it and had to take a picture. I still did not understand what I had to do with this situation, but I continued to listen and walk with him.

When we arrived at the place where he wanted to take the picture there were two people standing there, Les Brown, the motivator, who many consider to be one of the greatest motivational speakers who has ever lived, and Zig Ziglar, who was without doubt the dean of modern motivation, and one of the greatest motivational speakers ever. The photographer told me to get in the picture. I said, "What? Are you nuts? Those are the great ones. I don't belong in that picture!" The photographer said that I was one of the three speakers who had changed his business and changed his life, and he wanted to capture this moment for posterity.

I told him I appreciated the sentiment, but I didn't believe I belonged in that picture and in that group. I said, "Those are the great ones!" I told him he had to be mistaken and that I really didn't believe I belonged with the great ones. I was striving to achieve greatness, but I was not great. He went on to tell me about the impact my books and audios had on his life and his business. He said that my books and audios and Les Brown and Zig Ziglar's books and audios had changed his life and his

Les Brown (left), Zig Ziglar (center), and a young Willie Jolley (right).

business and how excited he was to have us all in the same room at the same time!

Again, I told him that I appreciated his words, but I didn't believe I belonged in the picture. He said, "Yes, you do! Please get in the picture!" I said, "No, I don't believe I do!" And he said, "Yes, you do! I believe in you! Please get in the picture!" I got in the picture and he said, "SMILE!" We all smiled and the flash went off and he had captured the picture. He said, "I am so excited because I have a dream come true. I have a picture of the three great motivators!"

That picture has gone on to become an iconic picture! I've seen it in art galleries. I've seen it in books. I have even seen it in people's homes, and it is titled "The Three Great Motivators!"

A few years after that picture was taken I was named "One of the Outstanding Five Speakers in the World" by the 175,000 members of Toastmasters International. Only fifty speakers worldwide have ever received that honor, with Les Brown and Zig Ziglar being two of the first to get it. A few years later I was inducted into the Speakers Hall of Fame and then a few years after that I was named "One of the Five Top Leadership Speakers in the World" and "A Legend of the Speaking Industry!"

Here is a lesson I learned. I didn't believe I belonged in that picture, but that photographer believed it. The power of belief is a powerful tool to help you achieve your greatness, and sometimes you don't realize that you have greatness within you, but I learned that sometimes you can go forward on somebody else's belief in you until yours kicks in.

One more incredible point that has resulted from this experience. Twenty-four years after the picture was taken, I got the call to replace Zig Ziglar on the national Get Motivated Tour after he had passed away. Zig had been the featured opening speaker on the tour for more than thirty years, and when he passed they said they needed "a great motivator, who was also a great man of faith as Zig was." I am honored they called me.

I'm here to say to you today, thank you for reading this book to the end! I say again that this shows me that you are a winner and I want you to know that I believe in you! So if you need to, move forward on my belief in you until yours kicks in. Keep the faith, and remember, I believe in you! Go forth and continue to pursue your goals with an attitude of excellence!

God Bless!

ABOUT THE AUTHOR

Dr. **Willie Jolley** is an award-winning speaker, singer, media personality, and best-selling author. He was named "One of the Outstanding Five Speakers in the World" by the 175,000 members of Toastmasters International (only fifty people have ever achieved this honor, including Nelson Mandela, Margaret Thatcher, General Colin Powell, Les Brown, and Zig Ziglar). The same year Toastmasters also named him "The Motivational / Inspirational Speaker of the Year!"

Dr. Jolley was inducted into the Speaker Hall of Fame (CPAE—Council of Peers Award of Excellence) and achieved the distinction of Certified Speaker Professional (CSP) by the National Speakers Association. He holds the distinction of being the first African American to be elected President of the National Speakers Association DC Chapter and first African

American to be elected to the National Board of NSA. He was named "A Black History Maker of Today" by the McDonald's Owners of America.

Dr. Jolley was named "One of the Top 5 Leadership Speakers" by speaking.com and named "Business Leader of the Year" by the Future Business Leaders of America. He was also presented with "The Legend of the Speaking Industry Award" by the Veterans Speakers Retreat.

Dr. Jolley can be seen on television nationally and heard on Sirius XM with his *Willie Jolley Show* and on numerous stations with his daily *Wake Up & Win with Willie Jolley One Minute Message*. He speaks globally to Fortune 500 clients and also speaks to churches around the world with his powerful message of faith-driven achievement. He resides in Washington, DC, with his wife, Dee.